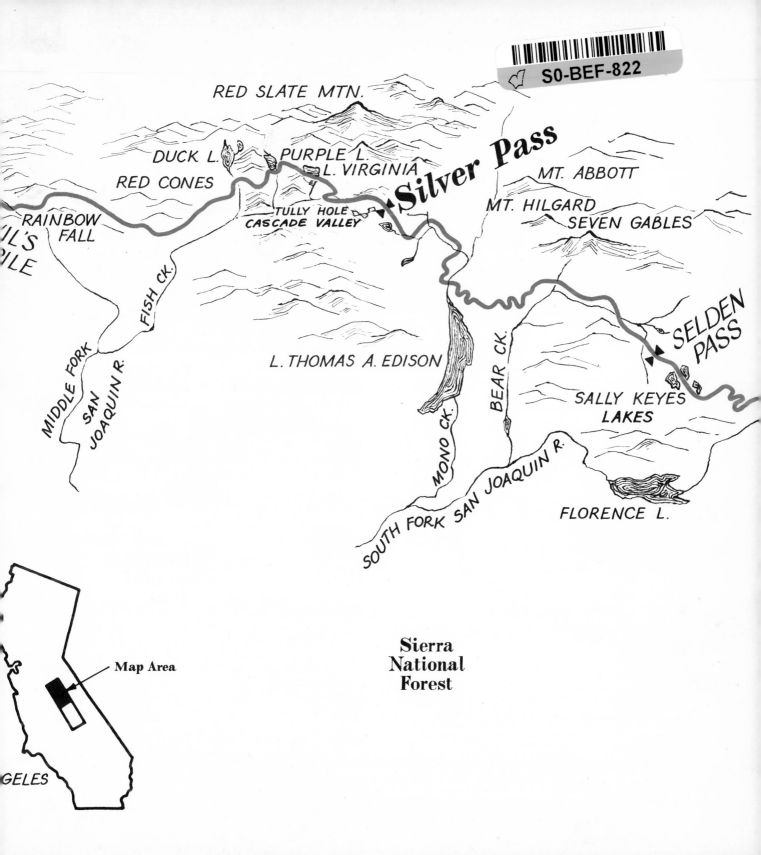

RED SLATE MTN.

DUCK L.

RED CONES

PURPLE L.

L. VIRGINIA

Silver Pass

MT. ABBOTT

MT. HILGARD

SEVEN GABLES

RAINBOW FALL

IL'S ILE

TULLY HOLE
CASCADE VALLEY

SELDEN PASS

FISH CK.

MIDDLE FORK

SAN JOAQUIN R.

L. THOMAS A. EDISON

MONO CK.

BEAR CK.

SALLY KEYES
LAKES

SOUTH FORK SAN JOAQUIN R.

FLORENCE L.

Map Area

GELES

**Sierra
National
Forest**

JOHN MUIR TRAIL — Northern half

PATHWAY
IN THE
SKY

Sunset across Emerald and Thousand Island Lakes, Banner-Ritter area

PATHWAY
IN THE
SKY

The Story of the John Muir Trail

TEXT AND PHOTOGRAPHS BY

HAL ROTH

BERKELEY   Howell -North Books   CALIFORNIA

PATHWAY IN THE SKY:

THE STORY OF THE JOHN MUIR TRAIL

Printed and bound in the United States of America.

Library of Congress Catalog Card No. 65-27593

Published by Howell-North Books

1050 Parker Street, Berkeley, California 94710

Contents

Essays which are totally or primarily photographic appear in *italic* letters below. Every attempt has been made to place the text and pictures in proper succession along the route of the John Muir Trail from the floor of Yosemite Valley south to Mt. Whitney. All footnotes will be found at the back of the book.

PATHWAY IN THE SKY
Introduction

I made my first trip into the Sierra Nevada during the summer of 1950. I went with three other men and together we toiled up Bloody Canyon — just south of the little town of Lee Vining on the east side of the range — to Mono Pass. It was spectacular, rough country with a crude trail that climbed between narrow, steep cliffs strongly stained with rusts and browns. The deep blue sky and the dashing white water of the descending stream made such a contrast to the cliffs and rock forms that the scene seemed almost too startling and savage.

The country was beautiful but the trip was horrible. Horrible because I had stupidly left the planning to the others who had brought improper, awkward, and ill-fitting gear from a war surplus store. We had far too much food and took along such ridiculous items as canned goods, cartons of fresh eggs, and *bottles* of pancake syrup and ginger ale. I well remember a pack with a metal frame that gouged into my back at every step and two small *suitcases* that blistered and cut my hands. But in spite of the discomforts I became intrigued with these wild mountains and wondered what secrets lay behind those smoothly rising ridges and spurs that ever climbed upward.

Back home I sought advice at the Berkeley Public Library where a cheerful librarian led me to shelves where I could browse in books on mountaineering. I found John Muir and his *The Mountains of California* and *My First Summer in the Sierra*. Here beautifully articulated and phrased was more than a guidebook or the simple story of a young shepherd. Here was the *feeling* of the mountains expressed with clarity and precision. I read Muir's other books and those about him by Linnie Marsh Wolfe. I discovered other authors. I found the *Annual Bulletins* of the Sierra Club, whose early numbers (1892 to about 1935) so well

typified the wonderment and delight of firsthand mountain experiences.

In 1951 I returned to the Sierra Nevada and with better planning and good equipment explored a bit of the John Muir Trail. Trip after trip followed. North from Whitney. South from Yosemite. Up the Kings River. Down the San Joaquin. Across the Kern. In time I came to know the smaller tributary streams and the little used passes. I usually walked and carried a pack but I occasionally rode horses and sometimes hiked with large groups. In my 15 years in the Sierra Nevada I have made many friends who have been generous with their knowledge and who have taught me to respect the mountains. Altogether I have covered the 212 miles of the John Muir Trail six times and made many side trips. But I am the first to admit that what little I know is only a beginning. . . .

So many people helped with this book that I scarcely know where to begin my thanks. The late William C. Putnam, former chairman of the department of geology at UCLA, spent long hours correcting early drafts and encouraged me in a hundred ways. Bill Jones, a naturalist at Yosemite, read sections on natural history. Dr. Robert Heizer of the University of California assisted with the material on early-day Indians. George Struble, Dr. A. D. Telford, and Dave Brower, though representing differing points of view, advised me on the difficult needle miner story. Mr. G. M. Spurlock, extension animal husbandman of the University of California at Davis, made me see the sheepman's side of early-day domestic flocks. Dr. A. Starker Leopold of the University of California, and Robert D. Metherell, Yosemite park biologist, counseled me on Sierra deer problems. Fred Jones gave me the experience of his long work with bighorn sheep. Alex Calhoun of the California Department of Fish and Game helped me sort out the intricacies of the golden trout story; the photographs of the golden trout would have been impossible without the assistance of the men at the Hot Creek Fish Hatchery.

Both Wayne Bryant, chief naturalist at Sequoia-Kings Canyon, and Dr. Carl Sharsmith of San Jose State College, who has pioneered such superb ecological studies on mountain meadow management, read and commented on many of my essays. Henry P. Berrey of the Yosemite Park and Curry Company cheerfully made arrangements for my varied peregrinations over the years. John Preston, superintendent of Yosemite, and John M. Davis, superintendent of Sequoia-Kings Canyon, welcomed me and introduced me to a number of experts. My great friends, John and Barbara Haddaway, made it possible for me to spend six months at Mammoth Lakes. Much of the book was written in Oxford, England, at the home of Hetty Hale-White who put up with my eternal typing and revising.

My many thanks to Tom Hamil of Pacific Grove who helped with the picture selection and the map work. The photographs on pages 19, 24, 45, and 132 are by courtesy of the Sierra Club as are the sketches on pages 21 and 36. The photograph on page 215 is reproduced by the courtesy of Bernard Clayton.

Finally I must extend my debt to William E. Colby who spent long hours telling me of his early days in the High Sierra. Then almost 90 years old, Bill Colby had close to a photographic recall of the early trips of the Sierra Club into the mountains and the first organized efforts of conservation in the West. Perhaps more than any other person, Bill Colby made it possible for thousands of people to be introduced to the pleasures and rewards of wilderness travel. As a young man he was a good friend of John Muir as well as dozens of other notables. For example he knew John B. Lembert who pioneered a homestead in Tuolumne Meadows in 1885. It was a remarkable experience to sit at the feet of Colby in his home in Big Sur and listen to the stories that Lembert had told Colby 65 years ago.

My thanks to all the others who helped.

HAL ROTH

Sausalito, California
June, 1965

1

HISTORY
The Magic World

High among the granite spires of California's Sierra Nevada, far above the thinning green of timberline, a single file of hikers heads south on a trail, looking from a distance like ants tiptoeing along a thread raveled on the edge of the sky. On both sides of the hikers we see the stony mountains pushing still higher. Patches of snow and great boulders cling to steep perilous slopes which gradually level out down toward the trail that slowly zigzags ahead. Far below, a necklace of lakes — still and metallic in the shadows — leads toward a distant meadow, hemmed in by encircling brush and scrub pines.

Closer to the hikers now, we see the warm, early morning sun shining golden in their faces. They step along smartly for the dawn air is brisk. It feels good to reach out with the legs on the trail after long hours in down-filled sleeping bags. The hikers are curious and they continually peer ahead, for though they know the way has been carefully mapped and the trail will certainly lead to the next camp, these wool-shirted walkers feel like explorers in a vast, primitive world.

They pause and dip their cups in an icy trickle tumbling from a snowfield, and for a moment, their voices silent, the only sounds are their heavy breathing and the gurgle of the water. The light from the bright cobalt sky, the glare from the snow, and the scintillating browns and yellows from the surrounding masses of bare rock illuminate the scene with such forcefulness that the hikers' senses can scarcely comprehend the hugeness of the landscape about them, until unbelieving, but still experiencing, they hurry on, their boots clattering along the rocky trail, their nostrils dilated from the moist coolness, their cheeks flushed with pink, and their hearts pounding.

"It's all so big up here," says a young girl, hunching her back and shifting her rucksack

slightly. "It's like the beginning of the earth must have been. Look at those enormous mountains and all that snow. And there's so much sky. I've never seen a place so big. I've never felt so small."

If one were to view the Sierra Nevada from a point high in the California sky, he would see a range of mountains shaped like an enormous prehistoric fish. This strange creature would be headed slightly west of north with its bony mouth at Lassen Peak in the north, its heavily scaled body reaching south along the California-Nevada border, and its tapering tail disappearing into the desert south of Walker Pass. In all, the fish would be 400 miles long and 40 to 80 miles wide.

The eye of the fish would be Lake Tahoe, near Reno. Its belly would rub the San Joaquin Valley in the west, and rearward from its dorsal fin the Owens Valley would mark its eastern limit. From our vantage point in the sky we would see the California coast and Pacific Ocean paralleling the great fish 150 miles to the west, with San Francisco Bay in the north, and Los Angeles just out of the picture at the bottom left. The backbone of the fish — to the east — would coincide with the crest of the Sierra Nevada which on the eastern side plunges precipitously to the deserts below. On the western slope — toward the fish's belly — the gradual descent from the crest slips easily into forested ridges and valley foothills. As our imaginary flight in space ends and we return toward earth we see that the wrinkled body of our fish has changed into gorges and canyons and peaks which increase in complexity and height toward the south — the climax of one of the greatest ranges on earth.

"High" and "wild" are the perfect adjectives to describe the southern Sierra Nevada. Here a colossal granite mass sweeps skyward from California's central valley to a rugged crest where 285 peaks exceed 12,000 feet, 140 top 13,000 feet, and 11 class themselves with 14,496-foot Mt. Whitney, the highest mountain in the United States south of Alaska.[1] The southern Sierra Nevada includes Yosemite and Sequoia-Kings Canyon National Parks, six major river systems, and thousands of square miles of magnificent national forests. No roads cross the range between Yosemite and the dwindling mountains far to the south.

The crest region — our special interest — is called the High Sierra, a land whose skyline is formed of sharply chiseled peaks that poke above expanses of bare rock, presenting a clean-swept appearance that would be far too harsh to be beautiful if it weren't for the glittering snowfields, the storm-tossed trees, and the delicately contoured lakes. It's a land of streams and waterfalls and glaciers; of mule deer and bighorn sheep and golden trout.

The canyons of the High Sierra are so deep and its spires so high that your breath hisses away at first sight. It's a land that mixes up the senses: the smell of wild onions, the ear-pricking howl of coyotes at midnight, the cottony taste of woodsmoke from a fire, the numbing of water when wading a stream. It's a land of colors that jolt the eye: the grays and browns of granites, the flashing whites of cascading waters, the rich reds of pine barks, and the crushing blues of dusk.

Altogether the senses are overwhelmed. You have to take it a little at a time to get used to it.

Though its very nature defies measurement, most of the High Sierra lies at elevations of 8,000 to 10,000 feet. It takes in roughly 6,000 square miles in an area 200 miles long and 30 miles wide. Eastward it nears the searing desert; to the west and downslope it merges into one of the world's most magnificent coniferous forests which clothes the entire western slope with pines, firs, cedars, and Sequoias at elevations of 3,000 to 8,000 feet.

Except for a few glimpses, it's extraordinary how little was known about the High Sierra until fairly recently. Because of its remoteness, difficulty of approach, meager gold and silver, and eight-month winter, it was almost the last part of California to be explored and mapped. The first recorded white men in the southern Sierra Nevada were American trappers prospecting for new beaver lands. These men crossed in 1827 on their way back to the Great Salt Lake after having entered California by another route.[2] In 1833, Joe Walker led 60 trappers westward across northern Yosemite; on the way the group looked down on Yosemite Valley and later viewed the "incredibly large" giant Sequoia trees.[3]

The few immigrants coming overland to California in the early 1840s wisely chose to cross north and south of the High Sierra.[4] In 1844-45, John Frémont and his party entirely circled the southern high mountains but at no time seriously entered the region.[5] After the discovery of gold in 1848, miners and settlers swarmed across the northern Sierra by the tens of thousands but totally ignored the southern part.

The main outlines of the Sierra Nevada were well known by 1850, but the remote regions were blanks on all maps. Walker had glimpsed Yosemite Valley in 1833, but it was not properly discovered and publicized until 1851.[6] Seven years later the great South Fork Canyon of the Kings River was visited by six men guided across the range by an Indian.[7]

The first proper reconnaissance of the southern Sierra Nevada began in the spring of 1864 when Professor Josiah D. Whitney, in charge of the California Geological Survey, sent a field party to investigate the high mountains and to seek out the sources of the Kings, Kaweah, and Kern Rivers. The group consisted of Professor William H. Brewer, botanist and leader; Charles F. Hoffmann, topographer; Clarence King, assistant geologist; J. T. Gardiner, assistant surveyor; and Richard D. Cotter, packer and utility man. The goal of the party was to explore, describe, and map the unknown mountains — or whatever was there — according to the best scientific principles.[8]

The men left San Francsco on May 24, crossed the hot San Joaquin Valley, and together with their horses and mules headed eastward into the sources of the South Fork of the Kings River.

"Along the crest, twenty-five miles east, are the rugged snow-covered peaks that we hope to explore," wrote Brewer to his brother on June 14. "The western slope is rough in the extreme, and both the topography and aspect are unlike anything else I have seen. The region is so *very* rough

CATHEDRAL PEAK GROUP — UPPER TUOLUMNE VALLEY.

that I am filled with anxiety as to the possibility of reaching it."[9]

The men gradually picked their way eastward, ascending through the forests and into the more open granite country. On July 2, Hoffmann and Brewer decided to reconnoiter the surrounding country from a high pyramidal peak that rose into the sky east of their camp near the Roaring River. Let Clarence King continue:

It was twilight of evening and almost eight o'clock when they came back to camp, Brewer leading the way, Hoffmann following; and as they sat down by our fire without uttering a word, we read upon their faces terrible fatigue.

So we hastened to give them supper of coffee and soup, bread and venison, which resulted, after a time, in our getting in return the story of the day.

For eight whole hours they had worked up over granite and snow, mounting ridge after ridge, till the summit was made about two o'clock.

These snowy crests bounding our view at the eastward we had all along taken to be the summits of the Sierra, and Brewer had supposed him-

self to be climbing a dominant peak, from which he might look eastward over Owens Valley and out upon leagues of desert. Instead of this a vast wall of mountains, lifted still higher than his peak, rose beyond a tremendous cañon which lay like a trough between the two parallel ranks of peaks.[10]

"The view was yet wilder than we have ever seen before," Brewer wrote later. "We were not on the highest peak, although we were a thousand feet higher than we anticipated any peaks were. We had not supposed there were any over 12,000 or 12,500 feet, while we were actually up over 13,600, and there were a dozen peaks in sight beyond as high or higher!

"Such a landscape! A hundred peaks in sight over thirteen thousand feet — many very sharp — deep canyons, cliffs in every direction almost rivaling Yosemite, sharp ridges almost inaccessible to man, on which human foot has never trod."[11]

The discovery particularly excited King who along with Cotter volunteered to climb eastward into the unknown. The older Brewer, anxious to know more but hesitant to allow his young men to risk their lives in such dangerous and wild country, reluctantly gave his permission. King and Cotter set off, each carrying a 40-pound pack.

It was King's habit to assault mountains directly, relying on bold frontal attacks and stamina rather than careful perusal of routes and approaches. Cotter followed King and the two men often got themselves in terrible positions — places they could get out of only by using a lasso to lower one another. For five days they scrambled up high granite walls, crossed rough-hewn spires and pinnacles, worked their way along delicate knife-edges and around huge boulders, cut steps in frozen snowfields with Cotter's Bowie knife, and in general subjected themselves to every test a mountaineer could devise.

On the evening of the fifth day the young stalwarts staggered back to camp, their food gone and their shoes in shreds. They had forced their way across the Kings-Kern Divide and back and had ascended and named 14,025-foot Mt. Tyndall. While on the summit of Tyndall, the 22-year-old King had swept the horizon with his level and had found two peaks higher, which he named Mt. Williamson and Mt. Whitney.

King left the party and returned to Visalia where he picked up an escort of two cavalrymen and made an unsuccessful attempt on Mt. Whitney by a more southerly route. The rest of the scientists — augmented by seven soldiers — continued probing eastward toward the canyons of the Kings River.

"It was a horrible trail," wrote Brewer. "Once, while we were working along the steep, rocky side of a hill, where it was very steep and very rough, old Nell, our pack-mule, fell and rolled over and over down the bank *upward of a hundred and fifty feet.* Of course, we thought her killed [but] . . . strangely, she was not seriously hurt."

Finally down in the South Fork Canyon of the Kings, the little group marveled at the immense granite cliffs which rose on both sides of them. They camped in a beautiful meadow and gorged themselves on the trout which thrived in the river.

"We left there the next morning and worked up the valley about ten miles," wrote Brewer that summer of 1864. "Next to Yosemite this is the grandest canyon I have ever seen. It much resembles Yo-

semite and almost rivals it. A pretty valley or flat half a mile wide lies along the river, in places rough and strewn with bowlders, and in others level and covered with trees. On both sides rise tremendous granite precipices, of every shape, often nearly perpendicular, rising from 2,500 feet to above 4,000 feet. They did not form a continuous wall, but rose in high points, with canyons coming down here and there, and with fissures, gashes, and gorges. The whole scene was sublime — the valley below, the swift river roaring by, the stupendous cliffs standing against a sky of intensest blue, the forests through which we rode."

The scientists continued to note the landmarks, use their barometers and theodolites, collect botanical specimens, and sketch the canyons and peaks. Their plans were to go north to Mt. Goddard but they failed to locate a route. Brewer then decided to cross to the Owens Valley on the faint trail of the prospectors they had met earlier that same July.

"Some prospectors had come over the summit to this place, as I told you," Brewer wrote to his brother, "and we resolved to follow their trail, assuming that where they went we could go. . . . We started and got about eleven miles, a hard day's work, for we rose 4,300 feet. First we went up a steep, rocky slope of 1,000 to 1,500 feet, so steep and rough that we would never have attempted it had not the prospectors already been over it and made a trail in the worst places — it was terrible. . . . In places it was so steep that we had to pull the pack animals up by main strength. They show an amount of sagacity in such places almost incredible. Once Nell fell on a smooth rock, but Dick caught her rope and held her — she might have gone into the canyon below and, with her pack, been irretrievably lost. We then followed up the canyon three or four miles and then out by a side canyon still steeper. We camped by a little meadow, at over nine thousand feet."[12]

Brewer and his men continued to toil over cliffs and canyons until July 27, when they crossed the crest and dropped into Owens Valley. The first scientific expedition into the southern Sierra Nevada was over.

The Whitney survey party had verified the presence of the mountains and had discovered a great many higher peaks than had been thought to exist. They had looked into the canyons of the Middle Fork of the Kings River[13] and had followed the South Fork of the Kings and the Kern River to their sources. They had climbed two prominent peaks which they named Brewer and Tyndall, and had observed two mountains rising higher. Their findings were put into Hoffmann's map of central California, published in 1865, which verified the locations of the high peaks for the first time. Brewer's botanical reports were published by Yale.

In 1865, the California Legislature refused further funds and the Whitney surveys ended.

Whitney went to Harvard to teach geology. Brewer took a professorship at Yale. King was eventually appointed director of the U. S. Geological Survey, and both Hoffmann and Gardiner became eminent topographers.

From 1875 to 1879, a U. S. Geological Survey party directed by Captain George M. Wheeler, worked in the desert east of the Sierra Nevada and established the positions of the high peaks Hoffmann had shown on his map. In 1883, Israel C. Russell, also of the U. S. Geological Survey, studied the glaciers in the Mt. Lyell area.

Aerial view eastward of the Silver Pass region. Mt. Izaak Walton (12,099) is in the right middleground. Red and White Mountain (12,850) is in the center background. The pass itself is on top of the ridge behind Warrior Lake, in the center foreground.

2

HISTORY
The Sheepmen

In many parts of the mountains the trails were roughed out by early-day sheepherders. In fact by 1890 there was scarcely an alpine meadow in the entire Sierra Nevada that was not known to them. Who were these men? What happened to them? Why have they been so condemned in the literature of the mountains? What is their story?

The start was in 1769 when the Franciscan Fathers of the early Spanish Colony commenced raising sheep at their missions.[14] By 1819, the total of 19 mission ledgers showed a record population of 186,233 sheep. But after the secularization in 1834, the missions were largely abandoned and the animals scattered. When California became part of the United States in 1850 there were less than 20,000 sheep in the new state.[15]

During the gold rush the hungry California miners ate all the animals in sight, at one stage paying from $7 to $16 for an ordinary sheep.[16] Large numbers were brought in to furnish mutton, the peak being in 1856 when 200,000 sheep were driven into the state from the Territory of New Mexico, the American Midwest, and from Chihuahua, Mexico.

The real beginning of California's sheep industry came in the late 1850s with wool raising. Fine-wooled Merino stock was brought in to strengthen the blood lines of the domestic sheep to improve their wool output. It was easy to handle the new stock in large flocks. They were extremely hardy and disease was uncommon. Land was cheap, there was an abundance of pasturage in the San Joaquin Valley, and with the mild climate there was no need for expensive winter shelter. Shepherds were recruited from Europe and paid small wages. The wool growing was profitable—especially during the Civil War—and the flocks increased rapidly.[17]

There were a few men who owned dozens of leagues of land and tens of thousands of sheep and who employed great squads of herders and became wealthy, but the usual arrangements were much more modest.

The term sheepherder referred to the man who was hired to tend a flock. His job was a lonely one in rough country and because he camped by himself for weeks or months in a small tent out on the range he was generally unkempt by city standards. He spoke only a few words of English but knew Basque, French, and perhaps a little Spanish or Italian. In an age when a carpenter was paid $45-50 a month, the sheepherder received $25-30, and was allowed to kill a sheep for food when necessary, besides receiving a supply of flour, bacon, beans, potatoes, tea, and coffee. His constant working partner was an expert sheep dog and he carried a rifle to shoot coyotes, mountain lions, or bears. With his supplies furnished and his requirements simple, he was able to save practically all his wages for his announced goal: a triumphant return to Europe to start a small business of his own. Some herders did return; a good many drank up their wages the same week they were paid. A few saved for land in the United States, settled and raised families, and became respected members of western ranching communities.[18]

In the 1860s farmers commenced buying the good land in the San Joaquin Valley and the sheepmen were forced to the San Joaquin and Coast Range foothills or to Southern California. Later there were further pressures on the sheep when the foothill areas were found to be ideally suited for growing grain and fruit. In Southern California the growth of railroads and irrigation made the land too valuable.

In 1865 a writer[19] pointed out that there were vast pastures in the Coast Range and on both sides of the Sierra Nevada where herds had not been grazed. He suggested that California sheepmen follow the custom in Spain where the great Merino flocks were wintered on the plains of Estremadura and the lowland provinces and were taken to the high mountain ranges at the approach of hot weather — usually around May 1. This was old stuff to the California sheepherders and owners, many of whom came from Spain or from the Pyrenees, where migrations up and down in elevation were the usual pattern.[20]

The use of the Sierra pastures was the main factor in developing the sheep industry in the San Joaquin Valley. Several particularly severe droughts had made this lowland unbearable in the summer and more and more sheep were driven to the lush highland meadows which cost the sheep owners nothing. Lean and weak sheep taken to the high pastures returned fat and strong. Often the herders went from the San Joaquin foothills across the range to southern Inyo County, then along the eastern edge of the Sierra, recrossing the crest to the west side in the vicinity of Yosemite Valley, or sometimes as far north as Lake Tahoe, and then back along the foothills or central valley to the winter lambing grounds.[21] Sheep raising became possible on a large scale and even though there was a general decline in world wool prices because enormous numbers of sheep were being raised in South America and Australia, wool was soon a principal product in Tulare and Kings Counties.[22]

Since animal pasturage was the only dollar and cents business in the mountains, a penniless 31-year-old John Muir, anxious to explore the High Sierra, hired out as a sheepherder. On June 3, 1869, Muir took 2,050 sheep into the mountains from the south side of the Tuolumne River near French Bar. Working with an assistant and several dogs, his job was to gradually move the sheep higher through successive belts of forest as the snow melted, stopping for a few weeks at the best meadows. Muir was horrified at the damage caused by the sheep which ate and trampled out wide swaths through the shoulder-high grasses and flowers. He called the sheep "hoofed locusts" and deplored the devastation they left behind. "The harm they do goes to the heart," he wrote in his journal. In beautiful Tuolumne Meadows he was aghast: "To let sheep trample so divinely fine a place seems barbarous!"[23]

In 1876, California's wool clip surpassed fifty million pounds. In 1880, the state had a sheep population of 4,152,349 — the largest in the United States. But with no grazing control the damage to the range was staggering. If the grasslands had been grazed in moderation they could have supported a fair population of sheep permanently. But the herders had little concern for the future. Not only did they bring in tens of thousands of sheep too many, but they took enormous flocks to the highlands as soon as the snow had melted, when the meadows were wet and before the herbage had grown up. The sheep moved faster on the short grass, eating what they wanted and trampling the rest. The animals' feet sank into the wet ground, cutting the soil and exposing the roots of the grass. Soon the ground was dry and bare in many places. Since the meadows were semi-permanent camps the sheep trampled the bedding grounds along with large adjacent areas. Each day the flocks went farther afield to feed, making rut-like trails that soon eroded out.

The worst were the sheep trails — one of the severest land uses known — where the sharp hooves of tens of thousands of ewes and lambs crushed the vegetation and soil twice a year. The plants were grazed closely and then trampled. The bare earth loosened and began to erode. Gullies developed along some trails until they were no longer passable at all.

Because of overcrowding there was a rush every summer to get to the best meadows. Men who claimed legal title to certain meadows or rented them from others arrived only to discover their grass gone and the soil harrowed to dust. "They found their feed devoured," wrote Professor William R. Dudley of Stanford University, after a field trip on the Kern Plateau in 1898, "and sometimes the marauders holding the conquered territory with shotguns." Dudley was amazed to find that in one year 200,000 sheep had swarmed over the divide through the Tule River region alone.[24]

The fact that sheep raising in California from 1870 to 1900 was considered a fast way to make money tended to make the owner — whether a small herder or a big operator—heedless of the effect on the land. Whether agriculturally naive or simply lacking in concern, the result was the same:

ruined meadows. It was only a question of time until the herders would be outlawed by the government or forced out of business by having exhausted the grass.

At least twelve responsible writers working independently in the High Sierra from 1860 to 1910 published strong indictments against sheepmen.

"The Kern Plateau," wrote Clarence King in 1871, "so green and lovely on my former visit in 1864, was now a gray sea of rolling granite ridges, darkened at intervals by forest, but no longer velveted with meadows and upland grasses. The indefatigable shepherds have camped everywhere leaving hardly a spear of grass behind them."[25]

In 1899, Dr. Marsden Manson noted: "The writer once asked an intelligent stockman how many sheep could be pastured on a given area in the Sierras, and he gave, as his opinion, that 8,000 sheep could be pastured thereon without injury — that is without destroying all seed of forage plants and grasses. But, upon naming over the owners and herds which he knew, there were 40,000 sheep accounted for in the area."[26]

"The greatest damage from erosion on the range lands occurs where areas have been badly overgrazed and the ground cover destroyed or seriously impaired," wrote the Agriculturists Sampson and Weyl. "Before the ranges had been overstocked and the ground cover impaired, erratic run-off and erosion were practically unknown."[27]

Some authorities thought the damage was more from mismanagement and not entirely irreparable. In any case the damage was done, both to the meadows and to the sheepherders' image in public opinion.

By 1890, the profit incentive was dwindling because of falling wool prices. Emphasis had shifted from high-grade Merino sheep to simple mutton types. The final blow to the sheepmen was the prohibition of sheep in the great Sierra Forest Preserve that was set aside by President Harrison in 1893 to protect timber and watershed lands. The Preserve ran along the west side of the Sierra Nevada for 200 miles and encompassed 4,096,000 acres. Rules issued in 1900 stated that cattle and horses were to be admitted by permit, the number to be controlled by the government, and no sheep were to be allowed at all. In the early

days of the preserve there were practically no forces to keep out the sheep, but control gradually came over the land, especially after the Preserve was reclassified into five national forests in 1908 and professional rangers were trained.

"The attempt of the tramp sheepmen to dominate the range resulted in such intense sentiment against them that the government was forced absolutely to prohibit all sheep grazing," said Will C. Barnes, writing for the U. S. Forest Service in 1913.[28]

✓ ✓ ✓

Yosemite National Park is perhaps the most famous park in the world. And proper is its fame, for nowhere else are such plummeting waterfalls, colossal granite formations, enormous trees, and beautiful upland country all exhibited together. When the park was established in 1890, it was before the days of the National Park Service, and the Secretary of the Interior asked the U. S. Cavalry to take charge. The park surrounded Yosemite Valley, then under state control, and was a very large preserve taking in over 1200 square miles. The boundaries reached eastward to the Sierra Crest, south to Wawona, north to include the Tuolumne watershed, and west to the San Joaquin foothills.[29]

People of today who calmly motor across the Tioga Road in an easy afternoon cannot realize what a wild and remote land the Yosemite High Sierra was 60 or 70 years ago. It had few maps and the trails were mostly old Indian routes. A trip to Mt. Lyell, for example, was a real expedition. The cavalry however soon established patrols to the boundaries of the new park and commenced working out trails and passes, and naming places and drawing maps.

Yosemite was established for the recreation and enjoyment of the American people. Mining, lumbering, hunting, and grazing were prohibited. There was no mining, and lumbering and hunting were easily stopped. Grazing was a different problem. Many of the herders who had used the high mountain pastures in the summer refused to recognize the new park and considered the High Sierra their own, even though they held no title to the land nor paid grazing fees to anyone. These sheepherders, and to a lesser extent some cattlemen, had run their animals into the Yosemite High

Sierra for 20 years or more and had an extraordinary knowledge of passes, meadows, and trails. They had nothing but contempt for government control and sneaked their flocks into the park when the cavalry patrols were away.

"The sheep-herders, few of whom are American either by birth, citizenship, or sympathy, care for nothing but the prosperity of their flocks, and where their herds go a desert follows in their wake," wrote Fourth Cavalry Captain A. E. Wood, acting superintendent of Yosemite in 1892.[29a]

In 1894, First Lieutenant N. F. McClure of the Fifth Cavalry, stationed at Wawona, wrote of an expedition "to scout for sheepmen, who were reported to be unusually thick in the vicinity of Tuolumne Meadows." McClure took twelve mounted men along with five mules loaded with provisions and headed for the remote upper Tuolumne basin. Near Mt. Conness he arrested four herders along with their pack train and had them taken back to Wawona. Later in Virginia Canyon, "I suddenly came upon two good-sized flocks of sheep. The herders fled up into the rocks, and we were unable to capture them; so I had one or two shots fired to frighten them. I do not think that they have stopped running yet. . . . On August 23rd I sent patrols from camp up and down Return Cañon. There were thousands of sheep running hither and thither, apparently abandoned by their herders."[30]

The cavalrymen were at a disadvantage because there were no proper penalties for herders who were caught, except to seize their packstock and camping equipment. The sheepmen talked grandly of armed resistance[31] and boasted of bribing soldiers with whiskey[32] but this was more bravado than fact. Under the leadership of able officers, the cavalry soon worked out the plan of scattering the flocks beyond the park on one side and putting the herders and their dogs out on the other, several days' journey away.[33]

"From June 25 until September 1, we expelled from the park 189,550 head of sheep, 350 head of horses, 1,000 head of cattle, and captured 27 firearms," reported the acting superintendent for 1898.[33a]

The herders fought back by hiring men to watch the cavalry.

"To add to the difficulty then this year, I found that the herders had established a system of spying," wrote Captain Joseph E. Caine in 1898. "A squad could not leave the home camp [Wawona] without the word being carried to remote parts of the park faster than the troopers could travel. Ten or more herders would combine in employing watchers, who were placed on the main trails to give the alarm upon the approach of the soldiers. By signal fires and other means the herders were warned to get out of the way. Lieutenant Kimball, who made an extensive tour of the eastern part of the park, noticed these signal fires every night, and also found warning notices nailed to the trees along the trails. Notwithstanding these precautions, many of the herders were captured, there being as many as fourteen at the home camp at one time."[33b]

Though the sheepmen resisted stubbornly, public opinion and the law were against them and they were gradually pushed out of the mountains. With the outlawing of sheep in both Sequoia and Yosemite National Parks and the restrictions on pasturage in the national forests along the western flank of the Sierra Nevada, large-scale sheep grazing ended.

A footnote came in 1917, 1918, and 1919 when stockmen "due to the war emergency" succeeded in getting temporary grazing privileges in the high mountains. These were cancelled after the 1919 season.

✦   ✦   ✦

The years of the sheepherders were also years of exploration for a few prospectors who sought gold, silver, or copper. At the outset, the difficulties of the long winter, ore transport, and getting supplies to any mines that might have been found would have stopped most men — all in fact except those with the glint of gold in their mind's eye. In spite of prospects from one end of the mountains to the other, little of lasting value has ever been found.[34]

An account of an early party prospecting for gold in the High Sierra shows the foolhardiness of trying to fight the mountains without proper supplies and preparation, and the difficulties of trying to force a passage without maps or scouting.

"We struck east," wrote prospector Thomas Keough, in 1864, "hoping to find a way over the Sierras and down again into Owen's Valley, but we could not get any further east — got into the main mountains and then had to back out and work south. We worked south until we got down on to the North Fork of King's River. It was a terrific task working around granite cliffs and over great boulders with our horses. Beveridge and I got down on to the North Fork one day about sundown with the animals. The rest of the boys had gone ahead and had been fishing all day, but could not catch any. Beveridge and I coming into camp with the horses asked the boys what they had got for us to eat, and they pointed up to a rattlesnake hanging on a limb that they had skinned for supper for us. . . . We held a council and the next day slaughtered one of the horses. . . . We made a rack out of green willows and jerked a lot of him and roasted a lot more of him in front of a big log fire. After we got everything ready we divided up the jerky and roast meat in our haversacks and struck south. We picked our way along with the animals, but the country kept getting rougher and rougher — deep cañons and precipices, a terribly rough, bouldery country—all bare granite. One of our party got part way down a cliff where he could neither get up nor down, and we had to tie our blankets together and let them down and pull him up. It was a several thousand-foot drop down below where he was on the cliff. We never could understand how he got down there. For two days we tried to work south. Finally we got into a cañon full of boulders, where we could neither get our horses one way or the other. They were so worn out and hungry that we finally killed them. They would have starved to death in that barren granite. We left our saddles and everything, and took only our clothes and necessary blankets and went on afoot. We lived entirely on horse meat. I don't know how horse meat might be with a little salt, but it certainly is not very nice without salt. . . .

"Traveling without the animals was easier, but the country kept getting even more impassable. In working down into one cañon, thousands of feet deep, we had to slide down a water-run. Sometimes we would slide thirty feet and fetch up on a bench, throwing our blankets on ahead. We camped down in one of these cañons one night and the next morning, started east in the hope of reaching the summit of the Sierra Nevada at a place where we could go down the easterly cliffs into the Owen's Valley. By night we had reached the summit at a place they now call 'Taboose Pass', about eighteen miles north of Independence, and the next day we worked our way down the east cliff of the Sierras along Taboose Creek into Owen's Valley."[35]

3

HISTORY
John Muir, the Shepherd of the Wilderness

Of all the men who influenced people's attitudes toward mountains and the out-of-doors, no one has had more effect than John Muir, a shy, slight-figured, largely self-taught mountaineer who startled the scientific world with his discoveries about glaciers in the 1870s, and who has helped millions of ordinary people see new values in nature by his keen observations on plants, animals, and the wilderness world. Muir, more than any other man, helped bring about the National Park System of the United States.

Muir was born in Dunbar, Scotland, in 1838. When he was 11 his father brought his wife and the seven children to the United States where he settled on 80 acres near the Fox River in Wisconsin. Muir's father was intensely religious in the stern mold of that time and the children had a severe upbringing on a frontier farm.

During the early years of the Civil War, Muir studied geology, chemistry, and botany at the University of Wisconsin. All through his youth he designed machines — fire-starting devices, a double rotary saw, sensitive recording thermometers — dividing his leisure hours between long walks in the woods and inventing. He built one of history's more drastic alarm clocks, a device that dumped its occupant out of bed at five o'clock in the morning. Full of energy, Muir was restless at the University and left after 2½ years to go on an eight-month botanizing expedition in the wilderness around the Great Lakes. In the autumn of 1864, out of money and with winter coming on, he took a job in a rake factory in Buffalo. With his clever ideas and hard work he soon had production increased to phenomenal levels.

But a fire wiped out the factory and his percentage of the profits and he went to Indianapolis to work for a carriage manufacturer. His aptitudes and a series of ingenious improvements in machinery soon led him to a good position. One night he worked late adjusting a belt on a machine and a slender, sharp file slipped and flew into his right eye, piercing the edge of the cornea. When he lifted the lid of the injured eye, the milk-white aqueous humor dripped into his hand. He could see nothing but black. "My right eye is gone!" Muir exclaimed in horror. "Closed forever on all God's beauty."[36]

The family doctor thought the eye finished, but a specialist assured his badly shaken patient that in time the aqueous humor would return and though weakened, the vision would come back. With his good left eye and the healed right eye, John would be able to see perfectly well.

Muir had to lie in a darkened room for a month while his eyesight mended. Many friends visited him but he had plenty of time to himself. He thought of the long walks in the woods, the wonderful wild flowers, the secrets of wild places. He thought of the trees and plants he had seen in Canada. He dreamed of exploring the Amazon. Somewhere he had gotten an illustrated brochure about Yosemite and he wanted to see the lovely Sierra valley.

Muir came to realize that his world lay in the out-of-doors, with wild nature, not with machinery and belts and saws. He made his decision. He would be a naturalist. "God has to nearly kill us sometimes, to teach us lessons," he said.[37]

Muir arrived in San Francisco on March 28, 1868, and set off for the Sierra Nevada where he was exultant at seeing the great cliffs of Yosemite and the grassy meadows and streams. His first awareness of the High Sierra came in 1869 when he herded a large flock of sheep into the Tuolumne country north of Yosemite. One July morning he examined some shiny granite outcroppings with his magnifying glass and saw parallel scratches inclined to the northeast. He noticed that the boulders around him were of different color and composition from the rock outcroppings and had been carried from elsewhere. Suddenly he thought of a glacier bringing the boulders from afar and scratching and polishing the granite on which he sat. "A fine discovery this!" he wrote in his journal.[38]

Muir subsequently supported himself by odd jobs but his exploration of the Sierra Nevada began in earnest. For six years he ranged over the mountains, from north to south, from the western foothills to the pumice craters far to the east. He traced rivers to their topmost fountains, pioneered routes up unclimbed mountains, and grew to love the stormy winters and the warm, flowery summers. He often went on long solitary journeys with nothing but tea, a sack of bread, and a notebook. He became a sure-footed mountaineer, often taking incredible risks, but somehow pulling through.

While making the first ascent of Mt. Ritter in 1871, Muir picked his way upward above the north ridge, worked around the highest lake, and climbed past the glacier. He followed up slim cracks, using tiny footholds, and climbed up and up until suddenly he found himself stopped with his arms outstretched, unable to go up or down. Below was the steep rock face he had inched his way up and down which he threatened to slip. Above was smooth rock.

"Suddenly, my danger broke upon me," he wrote later. "Faith and hope failed, suffered eclipse. Cold sweat broke out. My senses filled as with smoke. I was alone, cut off from all affinity. Would I fall to the glacier below? Well, no matter. . . . Then as if my body, finding the ordinary dominion of mind insufficient, pushed it aside, I became possessed of a new sense. My quivering nerves, taken over by my other self, instinct, or guardian angel — call it what you will, became inflexible. My eyes became preternaturally clear, and every rift, flaw, niche, and tablet in the cliff ahead, were seen as through a microscope. At any rate the danger was safely passed, I scarce know how, and shortly after noon I leaped with wild freedom, into the sunlight upon the highest crag of the summit. Had I been borne aloft upon wings, my deliverance could not have been more complete."[39]

During his Sierra years Muir continued to follow the paths of the ancient glaciers by tracing glacial polish, fragmentary moraines, and transported rocks. One sunshiny day in early October, 1871, while hiking in the Upper Merced Basin, in the shadows of Red and Merced Peaks, he noticed a suspension of fine gray silt in a small stream. "Glacial mud! A living glacier!" he exclaimed[40] as he got down on his knees and ran the silt through his fingers. He quickly followed up the small stream to the north flank of Merced Peak and climbed over a moraine. Before him lay a real glacier in the shadow of the mountain!

The first article Muir wrote was titled: "Death of a Glacier" which he mailed to the New York *Tribune*. He was astonished when it was paid for and published on December 5, 1871. The *Overland Monthly* bought two articles and Muir began to think of writing for a living. By the spring of 1873, Muir had 15 articles in preparation and had become a leading contributor to the *Overland*

Pencil sketch from one of Muir's journals showing a portion of the left bank of the channel of the South Lyell Glacier, near the mouth of the Cathedral tributary.

Monthly and prominent newspapers. Later he wrote for *Harper's*.

Muir continued to explore the Sierra Nevada. In all he discovered 65 small glaciers and began a series of measurements with stakes to determine the rate of movement of several of the larger bodies of ice. As his knowledge and writings and correspondence grew, he began to be visited by such eminent men as Emerson, Tyndall, Asa Gray, and John Torrey, all of whom listened respectfully to the bearded Scot.

Geologists of the 1860s and 1870s believed that Yosemite Valley was created during a stupendous cataclysm which caused the bottom of the valley to sink to an unknown depth and leave the great cliffs and walls suddenly fully formed. "A more absurd theory was never advanced than that by which it was sought to ascribe to glaciers the sawing out of these vertical walls and the rounding of the domes," wrote Professor J. D. Whitney in his 1869 *Yosemite Guide-Book.* "Nothing more unlike the real work of ice, as exhibited in the Alps, could be found. Besides, there is no reason to suppose, or at least no proof, that glaciers have ever occupied the Valley or any portion of it . . . so that this theory, based on entire ignorance of the whole

subject, may be dropped without wasting any more time upon it."[41]

Muir knew differently. He saw that the mountain landscapes had been created by glaciers which had scooped out lake basins, ground out valleys, transported material dozens of miles, and reshaped river drainages. The glaciers were the forces responsible for the final condition of the Sierra Nevada.

Muir continued to point out indisputable glacial evidence. The prominent geologist Joseph LeConte met Muir and was astonished by his work — especially since Muir's knowledge was based on firsthand observations and extensive field studies.

In those days geology was a young science and much that Muir wrote had not been treated in textbooks. He clearly recognized both ice-carved land and areas that had not been shaped by glacial flow. He traced the paths of the major glaciers and showed where they separated and joined. Muir understood fully that the ice flow which came down Tuolumne Meadows, for example, split in two and one branch crossed over a 500-foot divide to flow down into what is now Tenaya Lake and thence down Tenaya Canyon to join the Merced Glacier coming from another drainage basin. He demonstrated that the great Yosemite-like canyons always occurred at the confluence of two or more glacial streams, and that the size, number, and steepness of flow of the glaciers was directly proportional to the depth and width of the canyons.[45]

Muir pointed out to geologists that ice was not an unyielding solid when in a mass the size of a glacier but behaved in many ways as a viscous fluid which not only flowed downhill but also traveled over divides and ridges hundreds of feet high. He was among the first to realize the enormous volume of rock that was quarried from the Sierra Nevada by the glaciers and how much sculpturing was done by the ice.

By the measure of today's geological knowledge we know that Muir overestimated the extent of the ice in the Sierra Nevada. He was not aware of multiple glaciation and he made little allowance for stream erosion, but his contributions to the science of glacial erosion added materially to our basic understanding of the earth and how its landscapes were formed. His major articles on glaciation were published in the *Overland Monthly* in 1875.

That same spring, perhaps commencing too early in the year, Muir and a friend, Jerome Fay, climbed Mt. Shasta to make barometric observations. While they were on the 14,162-foot summit a blinding hailstorm suddenly swept around them. The temperature plunged below zero. Fay feared the dangerous climb down the mile-and-a-half wind-swept ridge and ice slopes in the now-roaring blizzard and darkness. The two men sought refuge at a sulphurous hot spring near the summit and for 13 hours they lay close to the boiling mud to keep themselves from freezing to death. Almost cooked on one side while freezing on the other, the men turned first one way and then the other through the interminable night. They could scarcely breathe through the acrid fumes from the gas vents and were in constant danger of being scalded by the boiling mud.

"At length, after the temperature was somewhat mitigated on this memorable first of May," wrote Muir later, "we arose and began to struggle homeward. Our frozen trousers could scarcely be made to bend at the knee, and we waded the snow with difficulty."[43] More frozen than alive, the two men stumbled down the mountainside to the village below. Muir suffered from the results of his frozen feet for the rest of his life.

Muir's reputation continued to grow and he was asked to lecture. Shy and afraid, he declined. More invitations came, among them one to address the Literary Institute of Sacramento. Reluctantly Muir agreed to talk. An artist friend commiserated with Muir about his fear of speaking and loaned him a fine alpine canvas and told him to hang it on the wall of the church in which he was to talk. "You can look at that, Johnnie," said his friend, "and imagine you are in the mountains."[44]

Muir was terrified of the large audience that appeared and when he began speaking he forgot what he had meant to say and was in all ways miserable. Then he remembered to look at the painting. Suddenly he was afraid no longer. The words poured out and the audience listened to a memorable lecture on mountain glaciers, a talk that began a long speaking career.

In 1879, Muir made his first trip to Alaska where he explored the little-known archipelago north of Fort Wrangell in a canoe paddled by Stickeen Indians. The Indians told stories of an inland bay of ice and snow which Vancouver's chart did not show. Muir was determined to find the bay and he urged his Indian crew ever northward even though winter was near. Finally on October 25, through a pelting rain and drifting icebergs, the little canoe entered what was later named Glacier Bay. John Muir had the first white man's view of the colossal glaciers and icy fiords. For five days the group explored the frigid bay and the glaciers, one of which was later named the Muir Glacier in honor of its discoverer.

The following spring of 1880, back in California, Muir married Louie Strentzel, a pretty, grey-eyed pianist from Martinez, and settled on her family's big fruit ranch in the Alhambra Valley, 25 miles northeast of San Francisco. Muir leased acreage from his father-in-law and decided to raise Bartlett pears and Tokay grapes. He did most of the planting himself and as usual had phenomenal success, selling the produce for high prices and banking most of the profits. He worked on the ranch for seven years, taking only occasional trips to Alaska and the western mountains. Two daughters were born and John and Louie seemed very happy. But deep within John was a gnawing desire for the mountains and the wilderness and a realization that he must write and talk about what he loved and knew best. It was decided to sell and lease large portions of the ranch to give him the freedom he craved.

Muir's writings again found a large and receptive audience. No longer did he specialize in geology but nature itself and the beginnings of conservation. Few among the millions of Americans who visit the national parks and forests today realize the struggles that took place to protect these areas from man himself. Three-quarters of a century ago few people concerned themselves with wild places or thought of establishing parks. Muir was increasingly concerned about the relentless destruction of the great forests of the Pacific Coast by lumbermen. He worried about the tens of thousands of sheep that were churning the alpine meadows of the Sierra Nevada to dust. During six years in the 1880s, it was estimated that $37,000,000 worth of timber had been stolen from public lands.[45] Operators of private toll roads controlled access to the Grand Canyon and other natural wonders. In 1889, together with an editor friend, Muir made a trip to Yosemite; he could scarcely believe what had happened to his old home. A politically appointed state commission operated the valley largely for profit for the owners of hotels and stables. Hogs, cows, mules, and horses ran in hayfields plowed from meadows. In Tuolomne Meadows the grass had been eaten and trampled out of existence, and charred stumps had replaced the trees.[46]

Muir got busy and wrote for the newspapers. He published two strong articles in the *Century* magazine telling of the wonders of Yosemite and suggesting that it be made a park for all the American people. The articles were widely reprinted and supported by editorials all over the country. A bill was introduced in Congress to make Yosemite a national park. Letters and telegrams flooded into Washington asking for quick passage. The measure was signed into law in 1890. During the same year laws were passed to create Sequoia and General Grant National Parks in the southern Sierra Nevada, to keep some of the giant Sequoia trees from being cut down.

In 1892, Muir helped found the Sierra Club, a group of mountaineers and people interested in the out-of-doors. He was elected president, a position he held for the rest of his life. A few months later a bill was introduced in Congress to reduce the size of the new Yosemite National Park. Muir and members of the new Sierra Club worked hard and brought about its defeat. On the positive side, the next year President Harrison ordered 13,000,000 acres of watershed land to be set aside as forest reserves, including 4,000,000 acres in the southern Sierra Nevada.

Between his writing and speaking assignments Muir continued to travel. Once when exploring on the Muir Glacier in Alaska he heard the wild cries of wolves nearby and hastily retreated to a large boulder where he could use his alpenstock as a club. Fortunately the wolves went away. Later he slipped and fell head-first down an icy slope. Two ravens circled overhead and shrieked. Muir shook his fist at them. "Not yet, you black imps. Not yet! Wait awhile. I'm not carrion yet. Go back to your gray friends, the wolves, for your dinner. I was only sliding for fun. My body flesh is not yet cast away. I shall need it for a long time."[47]

The Mountains of California, published in 1894, was Muir's first book. It was an immediate success and he planned others. But often he had to put his long manuscripts aside and write for such magazines as the *Atlantic Monthly* on conservation matters that clamored for clear exposition and the thinking of a man who wanted some of the wild places left untrampled for future generations and who realized the economic importance of conserving watershed forests for the sake of agriculture in the lowland valleys.

In 1902, Muir took President Theodore Roosevelt camping in Yosemite and the two outdoor worshippers became great friends. It was Muir's influence with Roosevelt that advanced conservation so rapidly during his two terms in the White House. In eight years the number of national parks was doubled, and the acreage set aside in national forest reserves was more than quadrupled. Roosevelt, acting on Muir's advice, proclaimed the Petrified Forest National Monument in Arizona, after Muir discovered that whole railroad carloads of beautiful stone logs were being hauled away and carved into souvenirs by private interests. Shortly afterwards part of the Grand Canyon was set aside as a national monument.

John Muir (kneeling, at left) giving a talk on the mountains to a group of Sierra Club hikers. Undated, but probably around 1909. Note the fancy coat on the dandy at the left and the enormous hats on the women. Nine of the hikers have staffs, often thought indispensable in those days.

To the end of his days Muir continued to write about nature and to urge conservation of the mountains and forests. He was an unexcelled observer and wrote fundamental material in a style that appealed tremendously to ordinary people. A measure of his wide and lasting effect on the hearts of people is the large number of schools and natural features named after him. In California, Muir's name has been commemorated in place names more than any other person.

Like most intellectuals Muir was endlessly curious. He traveled again and again. He climbed in the Swiss Alps, studied strange trees in Africa, saw the Himalayas in the sunrise, and wandered in the gardens of Japan. He returned to Alaska, and when he was 74, made a long journey into the jungles of Brazil.

In all there were eight books, including *The Yosemite, My First Summer In the Sierra,* and *The Mountains of California.* Muir received honorary degrees from Yale, Harvard, the University of California, and his old school, the University of Wisconsin — quite an achievement for a 2½-year student. The man who had so often called himself "a tramp" had become famous.

When he died of pneumonia in 1914, after a trip to visit one of his daughters, he was composed and serene, a man who had accomplished what he had vowed to do after the terrible accident to his eye almost 50 years before. "As long as I live, I'll hear waterfalls and birds and winds sing," he had said. "I'll interpret the rocks, learn the language of flood, storm, and the avalanche. I'll acquaint myself with the glaciers and wild gardens, and get as near the heart of the world as I can."[51]

4
HISTORY
The Idea of a 14-year-old Boy

By 1890, gold and gambling were no longer the main affairs of California. Its boisterous period was over. The attitude of the Far West had changed. The wild days of mining and lawlessness had yielded to a proper system of law and order which replaced the vigilante committees and ended the terrible business of hanging suspected offenders from the nearest tree.

A railroad connected California with the rest of the Union. New schools and churches were opened up and down the state. Artists, the opera, and serious music were accepted and encouraged. Newspapers and periodicals prospered, and there was a surprising flow of creative writing. Stanford University and the University of California became important centers of learning with competent faculties, some attracted from afar.

When the Sierra Club was founded in 1892, it was from the two universities that the new organization drew its strength. Among the 182 charter members were many highly respected engineers, scientists, and philosophers who saw the mountains not as symbols of mineral wealth, pasturage, and timber, but as a place of recreation and challenge, where men and their families could find excitement, pleasure, and inspiration. But the mountains would need protection. A principal purpose of the new club was formalized in the by-laws: "To enlist the support and cooperation of the people and the government in preserving the forests and other natural features of the Sierra Nevada Mountains." There was — and is — no objection from the Sierra Club to cattle and sheep grazing on the lower slopes of the range. Lumbering was certainly a legitimate industry on the rolling middle slopes where the timber (hopefully under selective logging) was grown on land with good soil and ample rainfall. The Sierra Club campaigned to keep the upland High Sierra for recrea-

tion and to make parks of a few superb lower regions like Yosemite Valley and certain stands of giant Sequoia trees. The founding members thought that if the beauties and challenges of the mountains were widely known and enjoyed, then the mountains were sure to be preserved. The new organization began meetings and dinners, started publications, scheduled outings and hikes, and did everything it could to make the mountains more known and accessible.

A few years before the club was begun, one of the founding members had had a grand idea for a long trail.

"The idea of a crest-parallel trail through the High Sierra came to me one day while herding my uncle's cattle in an immense unfenced alfalfa field near Fresno. It was in 1884 and I was fourteen," wrote Theodore H. Solomons many years later.

"The Holsteins were quietly feeding, and I sat on my unsaddled bronco facing the east and gazing in utter fascination at the most beautiful and the most mysterious sight I had ever seen. It was May. The rain-washed air of the San Joaquin plain was crystal clear. I have thought since of an earlier May when John Muir waded out into that valley in a sea of flowers and first beheld his Sierra. I must have felt that day in my cruder, boyish way something of the awe and reverence that filled the mature man when he looked upon those zones of light and color — the bloom-flooded plain, the old-gold of the foothills, the deep blue of the forest, the purpled gray of rock, the flashing teeth of the Sierra crest.

"I could see myself in the immensity of that uplifted world," wrote Solomons, "an atom moving along just below the white, crawling from one end to the other of that horizon of high enchantment. It seemed a very heaven of earth for a wanderer.

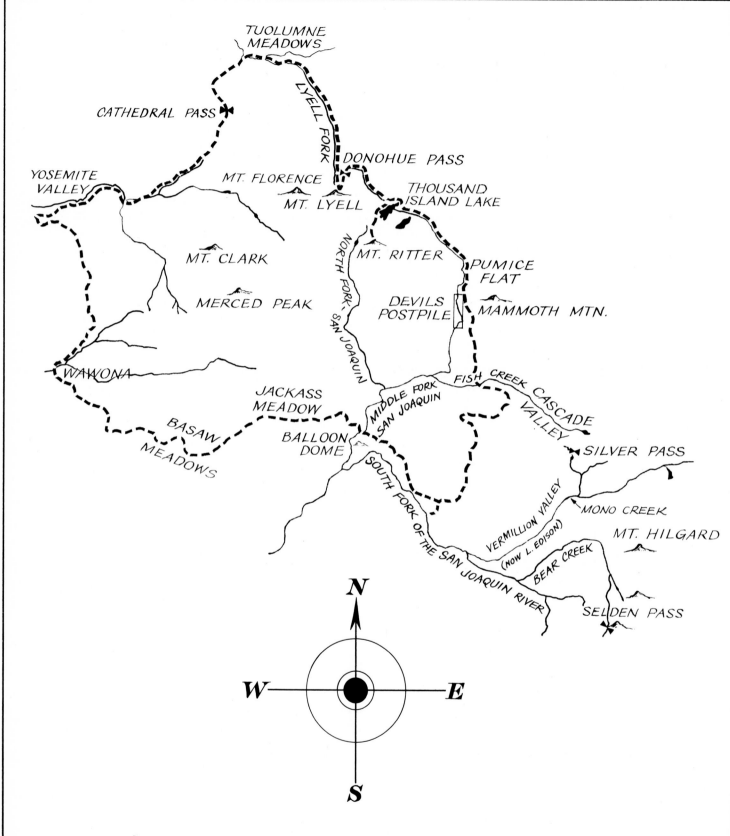

Solomons' Trip
1892 _ _ _ _ _

And heaven of earth it was — and will be until our new race is very old. I made up my mind that somehow soon I would make that journey."[49]

Four years later, in 1888, young Solomons spent a summer vacation south of Lake Tahoe, tramping about in Calaveras and Alpine Counties, enjoying the feel of the High Sierra under his strong legs. He liked his initial mountain trip, though through a mildly contoured, well-mapped area, and he dreamed of a full-length crestwise journey. But it took him another four years of working as a court reporter and saving his money before he was ready for an assault on the main crest, a wild and unmapped area whose main features and details were completely unknown. It seemed doubtful that anyone could make his way along the crest with an animal but Solomons was determined to try.

He and a friend arrived in Yosemite in late June, 1892, where they met Joseph LeConte, another enthusiastic explorer. In July the three men made a ten-day trip east to climb Mt. Ritter and then went down the rough east slope of the Sierra to Mono Lake.

Back in Yosemite, LeConte left the party, and Solomons and his friend packed provisions for three weeks on two mules. White-haired C. E. Watkins, one of the pioneer photographers of Yosemite, gave Solomons an 8x10 camera outfit and a supply of glass plates. Galen Clark, state guardian of Yosemite, wished them Godspeed. The two men left on August 9th, bound for the remote region south of Mt. Ritter which they had viewed on their July climb. At Cathedral Meadow, Solomons' friend grew worried about the lateness of the season and abandoned the expedition. Solomons pushed on alone with one mule, provisions, and the camera.

He worked his way south up the Lyell Fork of the Tuolumne River and climbed and photographed Mt. Lyell and its glacier. Then he picked his way southeast across a divide to the drainage of Rush Creek on the eastern slope of the Sierra, crossing what was later named Donohue Pass. Continuing south Solomons camped just above a shallow island-dotted lake, now called Thousand Island Lake, near the eastern sides of Banner Peak and Mt. Ritter. The next day he climbed Ritter, taking along Watkins' big camera and four glass

plates, the prints from which were widely published and hung, the first views of Ritter and its glacier ever taken.

Solomons found the view from the summit of Ritter to the south superb: "An exceptionally wild and rugged country, with many indications of remarkable scenic features," he noted. With his mule, Whitney, he pushed into the verdant canyon of the Middle Fork of the San Joaquin where he picked up an old sheep trail. He traveled southeast along the river until he crossed the old Mammoth Pass Indian trail and entered a broad valley where the river flowed alongside large areas of pulverized pumice rock. Here he was obliged to sort out a jumble of confusing sheep and cattle trails as best he could, frequently climbing prominent ridges and spurs to chart his course southward along the main crest. He took notes on everything, made sketches, and continued to use Watkins' great camera and the fragile glass plates. Day after day he went on. His food ran low — he tried to shoot a deer but had no luck — and he was obliged to stretch his meager stores by gorging on gooseberries and catching trout.

Solomons explored the region near the confluence of the three forks of the San Joaquin River and gradually worked southeast across Fish Creek. Sometimes the footing grew so treacherous that it even stopped the sagacious Whitney, and Solomons had to place the mule's feet for him. Striking south across Fish Creek from the confusion of "a million sheep tracks," Solomons finally topped the divide that sloped down to the great South Fork of the San Joaquin. For two days he tried to cross to the river—far below—which seemed to run in a perpendicular gorge of solid granite. Finally he left Whitney and his supplies and set out alone to find a way down. He worked through the forest and along the gorge monumenting his way by leaving piles of stones at every turn. After finally scouting a way to the river late in the afternoon, Solomons turned to go back to Whitney and supper—and found himself lost. He had not eaten since morning. His clothing was light, and he had only his compass, knife, and a dozen matches. With darkness coming on there was nothing to do but eat more gooseberries and build a fire and lie down for the night.

"In the twilight of the dawn I sat on a log waiting until it should grow light enough to follow the trail," wrote Solomons. "My eyes were sore from the smoke and glare of the fire, my face, hands and clothing were dirty, and all inside was a gnawing indescribable. The excitement of the night was gone. I was wrapped in the cold, grey dawn of another day, and the ashes at my feet were dispiritingly suggestive.

"It was soon quite light, and, pulling myself together, I turned in the direction of the trail," he continued. "Over a mound of granite, around a big yellow pine, and then I stood rooted to the spot, for there was Whitney, the pack on his back, dragging his lead strap, and quietly browsing near a pool. What a rise in the thermometer of my spirits! Let us draw the curtain over the scene of the greeting, which was quite too affecting for words."[50]

Solomons came upon a sheepherder who told him about a bridge across the river near Balloon Dome and — wonder of wonders — a trail to it! Two days later with his food gone, he stumbled into a camp of three hospitable sheepherders in Basaw Meadows near Wawona. The herders soon christened Solomons "The Photographer with the Appetite."

On the evening of September 10th, Solomons shook hands with Galen Clark in Yosemite Valley who informed him that his friends were busy organizing a relief expedition to rescue him or kill the bear.

* * *

Two years later, in 1894, Solomons again plunged into the mountains to continue south on the route he had pioneered. He hoped to keep between the main crest and the South Fork of the San Joaquin and if possible pass between the crest and Mt. Goddard, descending to Tehipite Valley and thence to the great gorge of the South Fork of the Kings River.

This time Solomons had with him Leigh Bierce, son of Ambrose Bierce, the acid-tongued newspaperman. The Sierra Club had been formed since his last trip and Solomons, always alert for information, had sought out and talked with John Muir. Although Muir had made no maps nor named any places during his Sierra years, he was able to give Solomons substantial information about the high streams and the crests they drained.

Unfortunately Solomons and Bierce spent part of July and all of August taking photographs in the Grand Canyon of the Tuolumne far to the north. It was not until September 1st — late in the year — that they headed south from Yosemite Valley with provisions for six weeks loaded on two mules and a horse. They made their way to the southernmost point of Solomons' 1892 trip, stopping on the way to eat mutton and discuss routes with sheepmen. The chief herder of Miller and Lux was aghast when he found out the destination of the two men. He warned them about early snows but Solomons and Bierce pushed on.

One night about two weeks after they had started they were camped in the forest above Mono Creek, one of the main tributaries of the South Fork of the San Joaquin. Their campsite was about 30 feet from an enormous dead Jeffrey pine that towered above them. They had built their campfire from its fallen branches and after dinner and the reading of some humorous newspapers they said goodnight and crawled into their sleeping bags.

"In the dead of night I awoke with a strange sense of deadly fright," Solomons wrote later. "A crackling sound had aroused me, and my unconscious faculties interpreted it. The base of the dead tree had caught fire, and it was falling upon us. I yelled to Bierce as I stood up in the prison of my sleeping bag, and had time to hop twice when the air quivered above me and a deafening crash chilled the blood in my veins. Something lightly touched my hair, and then there was again the perfect stillness of the Sierra night, and a pitchy blackness reigned.

" 'Bierce', I shouted in dread.

" 'All right,' was the cheery response, in a ringing voice, 'and you?'

" 'You bet,' I replied, getting bravely mundane in a moment.

"Moving my head, I found the thing that had touched it was rigid. I put my hand up. It was a foot-thick branch of the fallen tree. A few inches from my side there was another branch, and between Bierce and myself, who were not more than six feet apart, there was another great limb; and Bierce was hemmed in by them, as was I. He

Aerial view looking south up the Lyell Fork of the Tuolumne River. The mountains on the skyline are (from left to right) Banner, Ritter, Rodgers, Lyell and Maclure. Note the flood plain of the young river which prevents tree growth. Evelyn and Fletcher Lakes are on the shelf in the distant right.

had been similarly awakened by the warning crackle, but not taking time to rise, shrewd youth, had rolled in his bag about as far as I had hopped, or about six feet from where we had lain. Two feet back of us was the giant trunk lying across the canvas on which we had been sleeping. Stumps of its branches had pierced the canvas, and were deep in the earth. Seeking new lodgings, we finished our night's rest. In the morning the tree was merrily burning, telling us plainly that had we not perished at once on being struck by the trunk or impaled by its sharp limbs, a slow roasting to death would have been our fate. The branches of the fallen tree were so numerous that in no other positions so near the trunk, excepting the particular ones we had chanced to occupy when the monster fell, could two persons have been standing and not been struck. Of our many remarkable escapes during that summer, this must surely be reckoned as one peculiarly miraculous."[51]

Solomons and Bierce continued eastward up Mono Creek and found a wide, park-like valley about five miles long which they named Vermilion Valley because of the color of its soil. Turning southeast they forced a passage across a steep ridge toward Bear Creek.

"We led the animals a little at a time, each in turn," wrote Solomons. "When nearly up, the 'Kid' lost his footing in the loose, treacherous soil, and went literally heels over head, pack and all, down the hill, bouncing like a rubber ball from rock to tree, boxes of photographic plates the while whirling through the air; while the other jack brayed in sympathy and terror. The 'Kid' finally brought up against a bank of chaparral, and in a moment we were at his side, certain he had been killed a dozen times — jacks have more lives than cats — and so he must be quite dead. Instead, we found him in a sitting posture, winking contemplatively in the direction of the plains. Kneeling down, I reached my hand under his shaggy breast to the region of his heart. Heavens! it was thumping like a steam hammer. Though unhurt, the poor little fellow was evidently frightened almost to death. Singularly enough, none of the plates were broken — a worse fate being in store for them."

During the descent to Bear Creek the horse broke a leg and had to be shot. Bierce and Solomons re-packed the supplies on the mules and made their way to the head of Bear Creek. On September 20th, the two men made the first ascent of a 13,066-foot peak with a slanting roof-like top which they named Seven Gables.

From on top they tried to pick out a route for their animals from among the wild corduroy of peaks, walls, spurs, troughs, pinnacles, and cliffs that stretched away toward Mt. Goddard to the southeast.

"But the animal route!" wrote Solomons. "Well, our animals not being mythological beasts with wings, a glance sufficed to convince us that the Bear Creek divide was quite impassable. Yet, being within thirty miles, as the crow flies, of our destination, we determined to stick to our undertaking."

After two days of trying to work south, during which little flurries of snow whitened their campsites, Solomons and Bierce planned to give their two mules to a nearby herder and strike across the difficult divide on foot. They made up two backpacks containing the camera equipment, blankets, and food, which weighed 50 pounds each. As they shouldered their packs and led the mules to the place where they were to leave them for the herder, it began to snow. The next morning—September 30—they found themselves in a world of white—nearly four feet of snow had fallen during the night! "We were on top of the Sierra, some seventy-five miles of nearly waist-deep snow between us and the nearest settlements," wrote Solomons. As they debated whether to wait out the storm, the snow piled up deeper and deeper. Their sleeping bags were soaked and wood for the fire was becoming an alarming problem. There was nothing to do but to clear out.

The two men abandoned the camera and the seven dozen glass plates—on which they had lavished such care and hope. One mule had wandered off; they shot the second to keep him from starving. They left their flour, the sleeping bags, clothing, the gun—everything but a saddle blanket apiece, a little food, a few pots—and struck out through the drifts. Terrified by their slow progress and the difficulty of wading through the deep snow they kept pushing on hour after hour, their stiff blue hands mittened in socks. It took 2½ hours to build a fire to warm lunch. They stumbled on

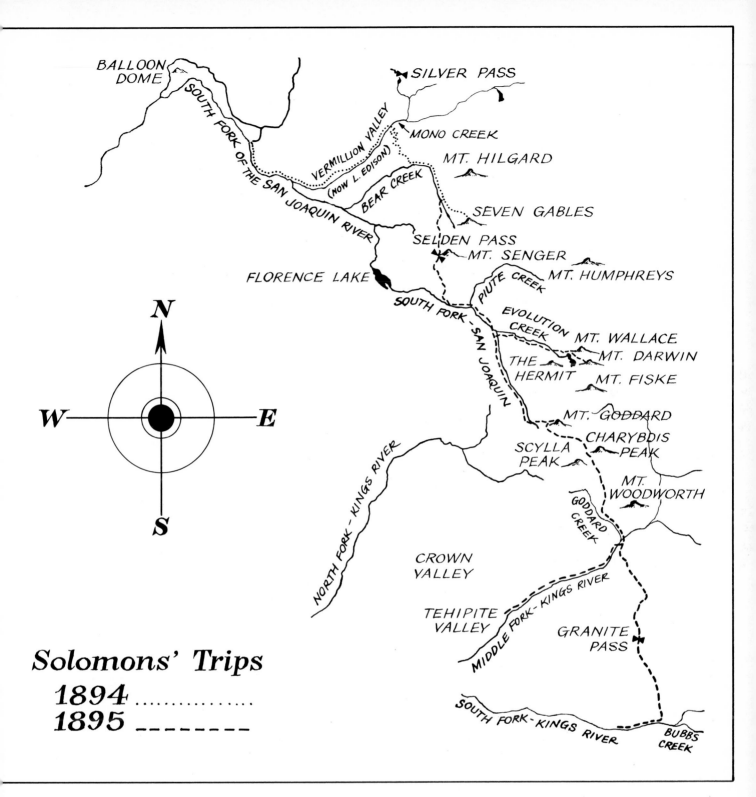

Solomons' Trips
1894 ·················
1895 ── ── ──

through the storm, exhausted from lifting their legs high at every step.

The cold night clamped down on the miserable explorers. They huddled in a tiny shelter scooped out beneath a fallen tree against which they had piled branches. Bierce got a chill and Solomons stood before the snow-blotted fire pathetically trying to warm the blankets and make coffee. At midnight the snow stopped falling. Bierce shouted and pointed to the sky; it was jeweled with stars.

The frozen men tore down their shelter and heaped it on the fire and huddled around it. When it was light they headed for the South Fork of the San Joaquin. The first day they made five miles;

the second day eight or ten; on the third day they waded across the icy San Joaquin. On the fifth day they found a sheepherder who restored their energy with huge doses of steaming mutton. They finally reached Fresno on October 8th, where they learned that the storm had been the earliest and most severe within memory of the oldest resident.

In spite of losing their whole outfit, including the animals and the precious glass negatives, Solomons wasn't discouraged. "As soon as circumstances will permit," he noted in his account in the *Sierra Club Bulletin* "the writer intends to resume the search for a high mountain route from the Yosemite to the King's River Canyon."

✓   ✓   ✓

In 1895, Solomons was again off to the mountains, this time with a new companion, Ernest C. Bonner, and a new 4x5 plate camera. After the ghastly experience of the year before, Solomons commenced his explorations much earlier in the season—at the end of June. He and Bonner went directly to Bear Creek where they found the remains of the abandoned camp. The big camera was safe in its case and seemed perfect, but when Solomons went to pull it out, it collapsed into scraps of wood; the glue had dissolved during the winter.

More peaks and ridges were climbed to chart the topography of the Bear-Piute divide. There seemed no way through and after a thorough reconnaissance Solomons decided that the southward crossing would have to be made ten miles west of the crest, in a gap west of a prominent peak he named Mt. Senger.

On July 12th the two men headed upstream along the South Fork of the San Joaquin from Jackass Meadows. Each wore overalls, a felt hat, two woolen shirts, stout hob-nailed boots, and carried sixty pounds of food and equipment. They climbed southeast along a sheepman's rude trail, their plan being to hunt for passes on foot rather than be held back by animals. On the second day they walked 14 miles, passing Piute Creek which entered from the north, and continued until the main canyon made a jog toward the south. Here a large tributary from the east poured into the river.

Solomons and Bonner judged the volume of the entering stream to be greater than the river in the canyon and set about to explore the tributary. The next morning they took three days' food and climbed eastward along the stream. They passed a series of falls and cascades and soon climbed into a valley which widened into a lovely upland meadow through which the creek gently meandered. It was a beautiful place, a paradise of tall grass, bright wildflowers, and calm water. Along the valley were three small meadows, each less than a mile long and surrounded by dark-green groves of alpine forest which gradually thinned out as the sides of the valley ascended in spurs and ridges of whitish granite. Evidently its difficulty of approach had saved it from sheepherders.

Near the head of the valley on the south side rose a large dome-shaped mountain of fractured granite that in its isolation suggested the name, The Hermit, which the explorers promptly wrote on the maps they were drawing. East of The Hermit six peaks knifed into the deep blue sky. "As I photographed and sketched," wrote the 25-year-old Solomons, "I felt that here was a fraternity of Titans that in their naming should bear in common an august significance. And I could think of none more fitting to confer upon it than the great evolutionists, so at one in their devotion to the sublime in Nature."[52] He named the fair valley Evolution Valley and the six peaks in honor of Charles Darwin, Thomas Huxley, Herbert Spencer, and Alfred Wallace, the British scientists who propounded the theory of evolution, and for Ernst Haeckel, the German scientist, and John Fiske, the American philosopher and historian.

The two men climbed Mt. Wallace and attempted Mt. Darwin, while mapping and photographing. Well satisfied with their reconnaissance into Evolution Valley, Solomons and Bonner retraced their steps to the main South Fork of the San Joaquin, picked up their cached food, and followed up the canyon to black-faced Mt. Goddard which they climbed and accurately mapped on July 18. Some eleven miles west of the crest they followed Disappearing and Goddard Creeks southward to the Middle Fork of the Kings, explored Tehipite Valley, and made their way over well-known trails to the great canyon of the South Fork of the Kings, arriving hungry and tattered on July 28.

5

HISTORY
The Professors Finish the Job

The same year that Solomons found Evolution Valley—1895—another Sierra Club member named Bolton Coit Brown began trips into the southern part of the range. In those days entry to the Kings River mountains was from Fresno and it took Brown three days of hard walking with his pack animals just to begin.

Brown, a professor of fine arts from Stanford, set off for the crest in early July. He wanted to climb Mt. Clarence King near the eastern extremity of the South Fork of the Kings. He left his animals near the confluence of Bubbs Creek and with only a few handfuls of dried peaches, a little bread, and chocolate, he scrambled up trailless Paradise Valley. At the confluence of Woods Creek he turned southeast, left the canyon, and struck out for the mountain directly.

That night he camped on the lower slopes of the mountain, keeping warm by covering himself with pine and willow twigs and building an all-night fire. At dawn he set off, ascending snowfields and working upwards, but he soon got into impossible precipices. He retreated, found another route, and worked along a delicate knife edge. "But it was all in vain," he wrote. "Presently loomed above me a vertical cliff fifty feet high—smooth as the side of a house. Only wings could go up there."[53]

With not enough food or time for another try at the unclimbed peak, Brown contented himself with drawing and mapping the parts of the South Fork drainage he could see. Excellent at making sketches, he soon had a remarkable likeness of the area, the first ever done. On the return journey he ran into a French shepherd who treated him to coffee, bread, and the use of a tattered blanket for the night.

A few weeks later Brown took a miserable little black mule named Jack north from the South Fork of the Kings to Granite Pass. They descended

The long spur of Mt. Clarence King from Rae Lakes.

to the Middle Fork at Simpson Meadow where the mule was put out to graze. There Brown disregarded the advice of all the sheepherders and headed for unclimbed Mt. Woodworth, set amidst great cliffs and ominous looking crags which rose thousands of feet. Brown followed up the southwestern spur, climbed amidst the jagged spires on the south, and surprised himself by reaching the summit at noon "after a delightful ascent."

He spent hours on the summit making sketches detailing the drainage of Palisade Creek and the Palisade peaks to the northeast. He climbed down finally in the late afternoon thoroughly intoxicated by the magnificent views. "This region is undoubtedly the wildest and roughest part of the whole Sierra Nevada range," he wrote. "From all accounts, it has never been explored. Even the sheepman do not go there, because there is no grass."

Brown hoped to work his way to the Palisade crests he had seen, and commenced toiling up the precipitous Middle Fork. He turned east at Cart-

ridge Creek and with infinite patience spent three days working up the short and terrible canyon. Jack fell again and again, sometimes rolling off the sides of granite slopes and somersaulting into space. Brown had to unpack the mule, get him on his feet, patiently re-pack him, and build trail by rolling boulders and kicking and smoothing the way. Finally they got across what today is known as Cartridge Pass and into the drainage of the South Fork of the Kings.

Ahead was a big mountain grandly pyramidal in form, whose summit was sure to be an excellent observation point.

"Of course, I wanted to climb it," wrote Brown, "but my feet were almost literally on the ground, rations were low and the future unknown. It worried me a good deal, but just before falling asleep I decided that it would be foolish to attempt it, and that I would not. In the night I awoke and saw its snowy slopes gleaming serenely in the moonlight. At daybreak it was still there—it called to me at breakfast, its rocky pinnacles beckoned me, its soaring summit challenged me. I could stand it no longer and hurriedly swallowing the last of my coffee, I threw prudence to the winds, flung some sketching materials and things in the knapsack, stuck the ice-axe in my belt and was away through the pines and boulders, over the roaring stream, through labyrinths of fallen timber and dashing water and nodding, many-colored columbine, almost on the run for sheer joy of that mountain and the delight of climbing up it."[54]

It was a simple but attention-demanding climb. On the way up Brown took his ice axe and playfully pushed off a two-ton cube of rock that was balanced on a knife edge. "Crunch! Crash! Boom! — the awful thundrous roaring down the horrid throat of the crevice — a far, growling rattle and a smell of brimstone; — it was a huge success." By midday Brown was on top sketching. He called the mountain he had climbed Arrow Peak, named Split and Striped Mountains, and made rough maps

and drawings of everything within sight — all for the first time.

He was determined to follow the South Fork of the Kings at the foot of Arrow Peak back to Paradise Valley and his permanent camp. But after three days of frustration with poor Jack—numerous rolls, falls, and somersaults—the mule began to fade and Brown got madder and madder every time he had to re-pack the animal. The canyon of Muro Blanco narrowed and they had to cross and recross the stream which raced over polished granite.

On the fourth day from Arrow Peak, Brown packed Jack in the morning and they set off on a trail Brown had carefully worked out.

"We had not made a hundred yards when he keeled over, and began turning back somersaults down the slope," wrote Brown. "That settled his fate. I cut off the load, got him on his feet, and headed back towards the grass. Opening up the pack I selected what I could carry, cut some har-

Arrow Peak, from the north. B.C.B.

Looking down Paradise Cañon, and across King's River Cañon. Drawn from nature by B.C. Brown.

ness from the pack-saddle, and loaded myself for a forced march to my old camp in King's River Cañon."

✓   ✓   ✓

In July, 1896, Brown took his wife Lucy with him and again set out for the Kings River. In the South Fork Canyon they met the party of Joe LeConte and the group traveled together up Bubbs Creek to Charlotte Creek. Brown and LeConte made the first ascent of Mt. Gardiner, from the summit of which Brown made new sketches and LeConte used his plate camera.

Brown and Lucy continued east and climbed in the Kearsarge Pass region and then headed south across the Kings-Kern Divide. Not since the Whitney Survey Party of 1864 had any reliable witnesses investigated the geography of this vast

mountainland. Brown and Lucy stumbled across the divide at Harrison Pass in a pouring rain and spent a miserable night huddled around a fire. About 3 a.m. the rain stopped and in a glorious sunrise the Browns set off for 14,384-foot Mt. Williamson which after moderate scrambling they topped by noon. Owens Valley lay 10,000 feet beneath them to the east, Mt. Whitney was directly south, and westward the lakes from which the Kern River drew its sources shimmered in the sun.

On August 1, Brown and Lucy named and made the first ascent of Mt. Ericsson in the Kings-Kern Divide. The same day the indomitable Brown, after sending his wife back, worked along a knife edge to another prominent mountain just west of the Sierra crest and left a monument with the name Mt. Stanford on the summit. His final tri-

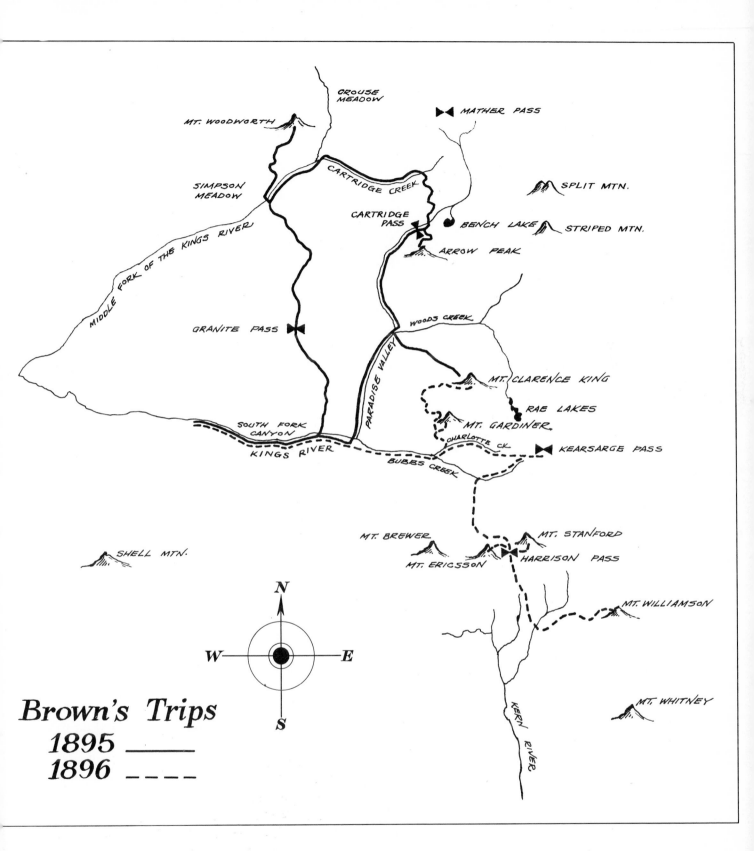

CROUSE
MEADOW

▶◀ MATHER PASS

MT. WOODWORTH

SIMPSON
MEADOW

CARTRIDGE CREEK

SPLIT MTN.

CARTRIDGE
PASS

BENCH LAKE

STRIPED MTN.

MIDDLE FORK OF THE KINGS RIVER

ARROW PEAK

WOODS CREEK

GRANITE PASS ▶◀

MT. CLARENCE KING

RAE LAKES

MT. GARDINER

PARADISE VALLEY

CHARLOTTE CK.

KEARSARGE PASS ▶◀

SOUTH FORK
CANYON

KINGS RIVER

BUBBS CREEK

MT. BREWER

MT. STANFORD

SHELL MTN.

MT. ERICSSON

HARRISON PASS

MT. WILLIAMSON

N

W *E*

S

MT. WHITNEY

Brown's Trips
1895 ____
1896 _ _ _ _

KERN RIVER

umph of 1896 was Mt. Clarence King—his defeat of the previous year—which he surmounted in a solo climb by going up the east face and doing some hair-raising rope work near the top.

The following January the Sierra Club published Brown's reports—as it had done before—including two sketch maps and drawings of the Kings-Kern Divide, the first public record detailing the region.

Three years later Brown was back, this time with Lucy and their two-year-old child Eleanor, certainly one of the youngest mountaineers ever to camp in the Sierra. The child rode in on a burro and enjoyed it all immensely, living mostly on malted milk, chocolate, and trout. "I verily believe she injured the fishing by her consumption of these last," wrote Brown. The family camped for two months, spending three weeks near Bullfrog Lake, high among the sources of the South Fork of the Kings. Brown was busy as usual.

"During this time I made several exploring trips into the basin next north of the Bullfrog Lake Basin," he wrote. "Notwithstanding its nearness to a well-known trail [over Kearsarge Pass], the inaccessibility of this country has kept it almost unknown, and, so far as I know, quite unvisited, until this summer. It contains from twenty-five to fifty square miles, is about as wide as it is long, and, after I had gone all over it, I put it down as distinctly the finest and completest epitome of Sierra scenery I had seen. Whatever makes the charm and the peculiar character of the High Sierra is here in typical perfection—peaks, walls, precipices, snow-fields, table-lands, gorges, ice-smoothed rocks, willow-bowered cascades, mountain-pines, columbine, and many other blossoms, perfect and extensive meadows, and lakes — ah, the *lakes!*—in every variety, form, and position—fifty of them if there is one."[55]

Brown's report of 1899 along with a carefully documented map and nine sketches was the first record of the region we know today as the Rae Lakes area.

✓ ✓ ✓

Though a dozen Sierra Club stalwarts contributed bits and pieces to the High Sierra story, it took a teacher of engineering to finish the job. His name was Joseph N. LeConte and he was the last great trail blazer of the High Sierra. He was born in Berkeley in 1870 and became a professor of mechanical and hydraulic engineering at the University of California. But the passion of his life was mountaineering in the Sierra Nevada which was evidently instilled in him at the age of four when he was carried to the summit of a peak near Lake Tahoe in the arms of his father. Or perhaps he inherited his love of the mountains from his uncle, Joseph LeConte, the geologist, who had traveled with Muir in 1870.

He started regular trips into the Sierra in 1887 and soon realized that in addition to sketches and explorations, scientific observations were needed. He began a series of triangulations of major peaks from Mt. Ritter to Mt. Whitney to facilitate accurate map-making. Together with his own notes he collated the work of others which resulted in a series of Sierra Club maps, culminating in his chart of 1909 which outlined most of the present John Muir Trail.

A photograph of LeConte taken at Millwood in 1908, after his most famous trip, shows a man of average height with a thin and wiry build. Clean shaven, he has large, wide-set eyes, heavy eyebrows, and a straight nose. On his head is a soft wide-brimmed hat. He is wearing a wool shirt and his trousers are tucked into knee-high boots, the soles of which appear to be coming off, typically the sign of a finished trip. The general impression is one of intenseness and drive which he must have possessed to a high degree for he made 44 extended trips into the Sierra before his health began to fail in 1930.[56]

In 1898, LeConte followed Theodore Solomons' route south from Yosemite. On the way he and a friend climbed Red Slate Mountain for observations with the alidade and aneroid. Further south they ascended Mt. Goddard but failed to find a way south along the crest, and detoured far to the west.

Four years later LeConte made the first climb of Split Mountain. "For eighteen miles to the south and eighteen miles to the north not a single one of the countless giants of the Main Crest has ever been climbed," he noted.[57] The following July—in 1903—together with several friends, LeConte promptly attacked and climbed two of the most notable giants—Mt. Sill and North Palisade. On top of the thin knife edge on the summit of North Palisade he set up his plane table and took his usual measurements of other Sierra peaks.

The main problem remaining was the crossing of the Goddard Divide to get from the South Fork of the San Joaquin to the Middle Fork of the Kings. It was of course easy to find routes away from the crest, for the jagged and jumbled environs of the highest summits made trail finding extremely difficult; nevertheless the very reason for the trail was to experience the grand panorama of the High Sierra so the explorers struck out for the crest itself.

In 1904, from a camp in Evolution Valley, LeConte walked south from Evolution Lake and Mt. Huxley, and passing Solomon's southernmost mark, strode into the great basin northeast of Mt. Goddard. The whole area was covered with snow except for two large lakes of deep indigo whose silent waters reflected the snowy peaks and the cloudless sky. Before turning back, LeConte looked down from the crest of the Goddard Divide. As he sat eating his lunch he speculated about the route that Solomons had dreamed of and wondered about the chances of an animal trip south.

"The other side, as I had feared, broke down in the savage black gorges of the Middle Fork region, which were choked with snow and frozen lakes far down below," wrote LeConte. "It would certainly be an impossibility to get an animal down anywhere along this part of the divide when the snow was deep, and even late in the season the success of such an undertaking would be very doubtful."[58]

In 1906, LeConte tried to close the gap from the other direction and pushed upstream along the Middle Fork of the Kings and reached Grouse Meadow. But he could go no farther. The next year, however, a determined U. S. Geological Survey party under the direction of George R. Davis somehow took a pack train over the Goddard Divide when the higher portions were covered with snow.

That settled it! LeConte determined to do the whole route. On July 1, 1908, he and Duncan McDuffie and James Hutchinson left Yosemite Valley, each leading a mule carrying 175 pounds. Moving rapidly they made successive camps at Sunrise Creek, Tuolumne Meadows, near Donohue Pass, Agnew and Reds Meadows, and Upper Fish Creek. On July 8th they crossed into the drainage of

Mono Creek and spent four days scouting and making the first ascent of Mt. Abbot. Two days later they were bathing in the hot springs at Blaney Meadows on the South Fork of the San Joaquin. Here they spent a day resting and washing clothes. Hutchinson celebrated by cooking a splendid dinner "and topped it off with a whiskey gelatine most artistically concocted."

On July 17th they moved to Evolution Lake where they prepared for a hard day ahead.

"The Goddard Divide was now before us,—the key to the whole situation," wrote LeConte. "If we failed in crossing it our plan of a High Mountain Route failed, for the great spurs and cañons between Mount Goddard and Woodworth Mountain formed an impassable barrier to the west of the Middle Fork of the King's River. . . .

"On the morning of the 18th we were stirring by earliest dawn, and long before the sun rose over the battlements of Mount Darwin were on the way," wrote LeConte. "We passed around the east side of Evolution Lake, and at its head crossed to the west side of the creek. The traveling was easy up Evolution Creek nearly all the way to the Goddard Divide . . . The gap was clearly in view, and we took our pack train straight up to it. One bad, rocky place was encountered, and soft snow bogged one animal, but the top of the divide was reached by about 9 a.m. We were 12,000 feet above sea level. Down the other side was an awful looking gorge in the black metamorphic rock, partly choked with snow. But there was no time to consider the prospect. We went straight at it, and took our mules right over the talus piles. They did splendidly, and we had cause to be thankful that they were so well used to the roughest of mountain work. We passed down into the rocky amphitheatre and around the south side of a little black lake, the extreme source of the Middle Fork of the King's River. The walls and the slopes of the large talus then began to close in, and we were forced to take our animals down the bed of the creek between them. It was a critical place, for a fall six feet high in the stream might at this place have put an end to our trip. By 11 a.m. we had successfully negotiated the first mile of the descent, and stopped to rest and eat a few crackers and prunes. Then on down the savage gorge. Soon the stream became entirely impracticable, and we were forced to climb out on the right (south) side over a little gap two or three hundred feet above. Here a stupendous panorama of the whole head of the Middle Fork burst upon us. We could look directly down the main cañon. Straight across the basin rose the spires of the North Palisades, and further to the south the wilderness of Cartridge Creek. The creek we had just abandoned dropped off in waterfalls hundreds of feet into the head of the cañon, and directly below were cliffs, so there was nothing to do but work off horizontally across the talus slopes, and look for a way down. By the best sort of luck this was accomplished, and by noon our mules were resting their bleeding feet in the little meadows near the stream again. We thought our troubles over, and so started at once down the east bank of the river, but were soon stopped by a sheer cliff 200 feet high stretching clear across the cañon. We had to retreat, cross the river, climb up the other side, and descend through a chute to the base of the cliff. Again we were obliged to cross, and so it went, first on one side and then on the other, of the foaming torrent, often crossing right in the talus piles, taking greater and greater chances with our animals, till about 4 p.m. we came to a meadow at the foot of the steep descent, and camped in a beautiful grove of tamarack pine. We were tired, and soaking wet, but happy in having accomplished our principal object."[59]

Day after day the plucky little group went on. The men continued to Grouse Meadow but failed to work past a cliff to upper Palisade Creek with their animals. On foot the trio climbed past the cliff and up the huge granite basin to the notch of what is today Mather Pass and saw an easy route ahead. The men were unable to get their animals up and spent two hard days detouring south up Cataract Creek to Cartridge Pass where they crossed to the northernmost tributary of the South Fork of the Kings. Two years before, LeConte had spied out a pass near Mt. Pinchot which they hurried over on July 25. A Sierra Club party had taken animals up Woods Creek and over Glen Pass in 1906 so the LeConte group followed their trail past Rae Lakes to Bullfrog Lake. The next day the cocky trio arrived in the Kings River Canyon and their great trip was over. LeConte and his party had walked some 300 miles in 27 days including seven days for peak climbing and finding their way out of Palisade Creek. Except for Mather Pass, the Kings-Kern crossing, and the trail up Mt. Whitney, this was the rough route of today's John Muir Trail.

6

HISTORY
The Trail is Built

No matter how good the artist or writer, no image or words can take the place of a real visit to the mountains. A friend can tell you of the rosy dawn over a quiet canyon or you can praise a watercolor showing bold trees silhouetted against sweeping domes of granite; you can read of big-horn sheep bounding across sunstreaked cliffs or admire a startling photograph of a spine-chilling mountain ridge, but none of these efforts can substitute for an actual trip.

To get to know the mountains you must sleep out in the Sierra night and see a new moon rising above a silent forest. You must feel the mist from a thundering waterfall settle on your face. You need to be startled during an afternoon walk by the crashing of a female mule deer as she bounds off through the trees with a pair of spotted fawns dancing after her. No artist can tell you what it's like to puff up an endless trail with sweat running down your back and legs and then suddenly burst out on top of a pass and see all the mountain world displayed at your feet.

People who know the wilderness generally want to keep some of that wilderness in a wild, pristine state and it was with this knowledge in mind that the Sierra Club inaugurated regular summer trips into the mountains. In the sixty-odd years of these trips, tens of thousands of men, women, and children from all over the world have been introduced to the wilderness, both in the Sierra Nevada and elsewhere, by various knapsack and pack trips. The first Sierra Club trip was in 1901, when William Colby took 96 people to the high country east of Yosemite Valley for two weeks of camping, hiking, and peak climbing. In July, 1902, almost two hundred people traveled into the Kings River Canyon (after days in trains, four-and-six horse stagecoaches—"behind clouds and oceans of dust"—and finally saddle horses). The following

year the outing group threaded its way into the drainage of the Kern. Gradually the summer groups visited much of the range, following the tracks of the early explorers to some extent. But the trail system of the High Sierra was poor, unmarked, and nonexistent in many areas. Some of the best country was completely inaccessible.

During the 1914 outing, Meyer Lissner, an attorney from Los Angeles, suggested that the State of California should undertake a program to improve trails in the High Sierra.[60] Lissner proposed a Sierra Club program to seek appropriations for trail development and he pledged his active support, which was no small matter since he was the political manager for Hiram Johnson, then the governor of California.[61] The directors of the Sierra Club quickly appointed a committee to work on the idea. John Muir died during this time and the secretary of the Sierra Club, William Colby, who was drawing up the bill, inserted the provision to name the trail in honor of Muir.

On January 28, 1915, State Senator William J. Carr introduced the bill in the California Legislature. In the lower house, the bill was presented by Assemblyman F. C. Scott.

AN ACT

APPROPRIATING MONEY FOR THE CONSTRUCTION OF A TRAIL IN THE SIERRA NEVADA MOUNTAINS TO BE KNOWN AS THE "JOHN MUIR TRAIL."

The people of the State of California do enact as follows:

Section 1. The sum of ten thousand dollars ($10,-000.00), or so much thereof as may be necessary, is hereby appropriated out of any moneys in the state treasury not otherwise appropriated, to be used in accordance with law toward the construction of a trail in the high Sierra region of California and connecting the Yosemite National Park with Mount Whitney and vicinity.

Sec. 2. The moneys hereby appropriated are to be expended under the direction of the state department of engineering and of the sum hereby appropriated, five thousand dollars ($5,000.00) shall be made available immediately and five thousand dollars ($5,000.00) shall be made available April 1, 1916.

Sec. 3. The trail to be constructed with the moneys hereby appropriated shall be known as the "John Muir trail" in honor of the late John Muir who has performed an inestimable service in making known to the world the wonders of the mountains of California.

There was a good deal of public support for the bill which passed and was signed into law by Governor Hiram Johnson on May 17, 1915.

Except for Yosemite National Park which already had a fair trail system, all of the trail area — save a few parcels — lay in national forest land.[62] Much of the northern part was passable on old Indian trails or sheep routes. Farther south the Forest Service had constructed a few canyon trails and Fresno and Tulare Counties and the Sierra Club had paid for improvements to other sections. But large parts of the trail were only general indications on maps with scattered monuments to mark the way. There were almost no signs giving correct mileages, proper names, and directions. In addition, trail had to be built from scratch to connect the San Joaquin and Kings River Basin via Muir Pass. Another link was needed across the Kings-Kern Divide. The appropriation of $10,000 even in 1915, was a small sum for such a big job.

The state engineer, William F. McClure, listened to the experts of the Forest Service and Sierra Club and made two inspection trips on horseback before establishing the exact route.[63] Since most of the work was to be on land controlled by the Forest Service, McClure asked its officers to supervise the construction. Not only did the Forest Service agree to manage the work, but it contributed the services of its officers without charge. The supervisors, district foresters, and rangers got enthusiastic over the project and achieved remarkable returns from the modest budget.[64]

Work was quickly begun and by August, two eight-man crews were started in Sierra National Forest and one farther south in Sequoia National Forest. The most necessary trail construction had been scouted and in two months a much-needed new bridge spanned Piute Creek on the South Fork of the San Joaquin, a trail had been commenced south from Muir Pass, and six miles of new trail linked the Kings River Basin with the Kern, via Junction and Shepherd Passes.

The official route was carefully gone over to find the best location for the trail — away, for example, from the shaded south sides of canyons where lingering snowbanks would cover the route until late in the year. Was the way through a talus field which would necessitate moving huge boulders? Would a steep cliff have to be blasted to locate the trail or could the cliff be by-passed by climbing above it? What about river crossings? Fording raging mountain streams in early summer is the most hazardous thing in the mountains but bridges are expensive in the back country where everything has to be packed in or made on the spot. And besides maintenance, there are snow, ice, avalanches, or high water that sometimes take a bridge out completely. A stream crossed on the way up a canyon often has to be crossed a second time by another bridge farther up. Nevertheless some bridges were necessary.

In early summer, soft meadows are boggy, animal's hooves cut the soil badly which soon leads to ever-growing washouts. A route should rim the higher drier meadow edges. A climb steeper than 15 or 20 per cent generally has to be solved by constructing switchbacks or long traverses. A forest trail may require the cutting of a hundred fallen trees and the blasting of stumps. Sandy places and meadow trails need fitting with rocks to divert water that comes down the trail to keep the path from turning into a canal. The trail builders tried to avoid slide areas and brush thickets and often built up high to miss early summer flooding from melting snow.

In an age when a glass of beer was five cents and a man's shirt cost $1.50, laborers received $2.00 a day and board. The foreman got $3.00 and board, and the cook $60 a month. The money of course came from the state but since the Forest Service was in charge, it was looked to for payment. By mistake one payroll was sent to a Forest Service man who was on leave. "Delivery of the checks was delayed until the rangers felt it wise to avoid the neighborhood of the men who had money coming to them," wrote the Forest Service official

THE TRAIL IS BUILT

in charge.[65] The payroll arrangements were improved however and progress on the trail continued until the October weather stopped everything for the year.

Building trail is a lot different than hiking or riding horseback over it. When you travel you have the challenge of the journey and the excitement and change of the scenery. But when you're a member of a trail gang your world shrinks to 200 feet of stone rolling or 35 feet of blasting. Your main tools are a shovel and pick. You pry large rocks with a bar and carry small rocks and gravel fill in a wheelbarrow. When you blast you drill into the granite with a star drill driven by a sledge, pack the hole with 40 or 60 per cent powder, and string the wires to a protected place before setting off the charge. You cut brush with an axe, and fallen trees with a saw. Sometimes you can use a mule to help drag rocks or guide a horse-drawn scraper along a forest trail. But usually the work boils down to a few men with simple hand tools prying, rolling, lifting, shoveling, filling in, chopping — a lot of hard brutal work — especially before the days of portable compressors for drilling into rock, and chain saws to cut timber. The trail camps were sometimes three miles from work because of wood, water, and shelter problems which meant a six-mile walk on top of a hard day's labor.

There were usually two types of men on the trail crews. The first was a college boy on a summer lark. He was strong and robust with a great deal of energy and if properly supervised and his morale was kept up was capable of considerable work. The second employee was a more modestly educated older man, a good deal steadier, who was often put to work during other seasons lower down in the park or forest. Each was a casual laborer however and apt to quit at any moment.

"The task of overseeing the packing of powder, steel, supplies, etc., over difficult mountain trails, and of handling men, the best of whom grow sick and tired of the isolation and monotony of camp fifty to seventy miles from civilization, is no small one and requires lots of patience and tact," wrote Forest Supervisor Paul Redington of Sierra National Forest.[66]

His counterpart farther south in Sequoia National Forest, S. N. Wynne, noted that, "It was planned to start work during the early part of

June. Extraordinarily heavy snow made it impossible even to get into the area until June 27 and the real crew work could not be done before July 4. Considerable trouble on the early work was occasioned by snow-blindness, and men were very hard to get and keep. Great credit is due to Thomas Adamson, the foreman, for continuing the work even when single-handed. A little later conditions were better."[67]

In 1916, the men built 3⅛ miles of trail in Center Basin and worked up the Middle Fork of the Kings River to three miles south of Muir Pass. The following year a new appropriation of $10,000 paid for two bridges across the San Joaquin River below Evolution Creek and additional work south of Muir Pass. A particularly severe problem was Barrier Rock, a great reef of granite that rose abruptly from the stream bed on both sides of the Kings River. To locate the trail, the crew had to blast half a tunnel in the perpendicular granite wall, drilling each powder hole with a star drill and sledgehammer.

New funds of $10,000 in 1926 paid for 17 miles of trail north from the vicinity of Selden Pass. Similar appropriations in 1927 and 1929 put new trail across Silver Pass, bridged Fish Creek, and ran a fine route past Virginia and Purple Lakes northwest to Devils Postpile National Monument. During 1930, the trail to the summit of Mt. Whitney was completed from Crabtree Meadows.

The same year, work was started on Forester Pass, a newly discovered direct animal crossing of the Kings-Kern Divide which obviated the long detour east via Junction and Shepherd Passes. Since the pass was the boundary of Sequoia National Forest and the recently enlarged Sequoia National Park, crews worked on both sides. On August 26, a rock slide after a blast seriously injured four men, one of whom, Donald Downs, aged 19, died on September 2, despite every effort to save him.[68] (A plaque to Downs' memory, erected by his fellow workers, is on the south side of the pass.) The following year expenditures of $2,000 completed the northern side of the pass and five miles of new trail was opened south to Tyndall Creek.

State aid totalling $50,000 had been spent on the John Muir Trail which was now entirely complete except for the section up Palisade Creek.

This uncompleted part had forced a long detour to Simpson Meadow, missing the northern sources of the South Fork of the Kings entirely. In 1938, the Forest Service constructed steep switchbacks up an almost vertical cliff below Palisade Lakes and built across the open granite to Mather Pass. Then the trail makers went south across Upper Basin, the area that Bolton Coit Brown had so carefully sketched 43 years before.

The trail was complete, 54 years after the dream of young Solomons on that May day in 1884 when he had ridden his uncle's bronco in the alfalfa field in the San Joaquin Valley and vowed to make a trip along the crest of the Sierra Nevada. State engineers, government survey officials, Forest Service rangers, men from the National Park Service, Sierra Club members, sheepherders, U. S. Cavalrymen, gold miners — all had had a part.

YOSEMITE VALLEY TO DONOHUE PASS

7

YOSEMITE VALLEY TO DONOHUE PASS
Giant Staircase

The lowest point on the entire John Muir Trail is at its beginning in Yosemite Valley at Happy Isles where the elevation is 4,034 feet above the sea. From here the trail climbs up the steep canyon of the Merced River, gaining about 2,000 feet in four miles and passing Vernal and Nevada Falls, two of Yosemite's finest water displays. Viewed from the nearby prominences of Glacier Point or Sierra Point the course of the river looks like a giant staircase. The falls are formed as the water tumbles down steps that measure over 300 feet, becoming rocketing ribbons of white that first spread and then coalesce, until they thunder on the bedrock below where the water boils and churns, bathing the bases of the falls in perpetual mists which encourage lush growths of ferns and flowers.

A first glance might suggest that the canyon was formed by the action of the river, but on looking closer we see that the bedrock is tough and unyielding granite into which the river has scarcely cut a channel at all. Four times in the recent geologic past, the earth has undergone extended periods of cold weather. As long ago as three million years and as recently as 11,000 years, tremendous amounts of snow accumulated in the Sierra Nevada. The snow was recrystallized to ice and grew to depths of thousands of feet in the canyons. Much of this granular ice formed into glaciers—huge tongues of moving ice—which crept down from the mountain crests at the rate of a few inches to a few feet or more each day. Since a single cubic foot of ice weighs 57 pounds, a thickness of 100 feet of ice exerts a pressure of more than 2.8 tons on every square foot of rock below. These colossal glaciers—whose bluish ice weighed millions of tons—scoured and abraded the granite of the mountains and cut deeply into hundreds of chasms and gorges.

Projecting masses of rock were knocked loose. Large boulders were embedded in the ice and acted like giant chisels, gouging into the hard granite underneath and in the process destroying themselves. Rocks were ground together and broken and rounded; some were pulverized into fine abrasive which smoothed and polished the granite that wasn't carried away. The glaciers widened and deepened the canyons and left trails of fine scratches on exposed ledges. The moving ice transported vast amounts of loose rock and whenever the ice flows combined, narrowed, or terminated, they left behind moraines—heaps of jumbled rocks and boulders.

The erosional effects of the ice depended on the resistance of the rock and the occurrence of natural cracks and joints. Wherever a joint or cleavage plane existed across the direction of glacial flow, the ice tended to split off, quarry, and remove large blocks, often carrying them miles. This process is known as plucking and is helped materially by pressure, freezing, and frost wedging. Underneath the glacier, meltwater froze on the bottom surface and in the cracks of blocks during periods of reduced movement. When the flow of the glacier resumed, such blocks—now firmly frozen to the glacier—were loosened or pulled out.

In the photograph, the topmost step over which Nevada Falls tumbles is 594 feet high. The next step down—lost among the trees in the picture—measures 50 feet, causing a series of cascades. The bottom step, responsible for Vernal Falls, is 317 feet. These steps are at narrow places in the canyon where the unfractured bedrock is particularly resistant and unyielding—situations that tended to dam up the ice and increase its excavating force on the more closely fractured rock below. The Nevada Falls cliff, for example, consists of massive rock for 400 feet, topped by a 200-foot upper portion marked by only a few horizontal fractures.

The remarkably clean-cut smooth front and the straight edge of the step show that the quarrying was governed by natural partings in the rock. The step front resulted from an enormous, vertical joint that tended at roughly right angles to the flow of the ice. Below the great vertical joint the rock was plentifully divided by natural partings and was readily quarried away.

The giant staircase that we see is only part of a much greater stairway that extends all the way from lower Yosemite Valley up to the starting point of the ancient Merced glaciers near Mt. Lyell, far to the east. The total staircase is 21 miles long and makes a climb of 7,600 feet. Though few of the steps are as clear and distinct as those of Vernal and Nevada Falls, the configuration of the glacial staircase is unmistakable and affords one of the greatest contrasts between a V-shaped valley excavated by running water and a U-shaped valley formed by a glacier.

The flow of water in the Merced River varies enormously from month to month. An average of 45 years of U. S. Geological Survey stream flow records taken at Happy Isles gives a flow of 337 cubic feet per second. May and June are the big months when the snow pack is melting; then the flow sometimes exceeds 2,000 cubic feet per second, as in 1938 when the charging waters ran 2,295 cubic feet per second for 60 days! The other end of the scale was 1924, when May and June averaged only 777.

Slack water months are September, October, and November, when the snow is largely gone. The record low is a feeble 2.58 feet in October, 1956. Unusual storms can grossly upset averages, for October, 1919, shows a flow of 267 feet.

My favorite part of the John Muir Trail is between Nevada Falls and Sunrise Camp. In Little Yosemite Valley the placid Merced River runs lazily along between overhanging trees and tall bushes, and reflects and amplifies the soft colors of the leaves into a shimmering effulgence of muted green. You almost feel that the quiet river is storing up energy for its crashing, dashing life over the falls below.

Near Half Dome the trail switchbacks up past dozens of enormous Jeffrey pines whose huge brown boles rise from a heavy litter of cones, bark, and old leaves — so soft and cushiony that you want to lie back and just sink down and down. And the western azalea and the ferns along Sunrise Creek! The perfume of the azalea is so lilting, sweet, and pervading that I feel like the little girl in the *Wizard of Oz* who could scarcely keep her eyes open in the poppy field. I want to sink down among the velvety green of the new ferns and stay there forever. . . .

8

YOSEMITE VALLEY TO DONOHUE PASS
Indian Traders

The earliest trails in the Sierra Nevada were tramped out by Indians crossing the mountains to trade. The Paiute Indians from the Owens Valley and Mono Lake region on the east frequently met with Western Mono, Miwok, and Yokut tribes from the west.

Both men and women crossed the range, usually barefoot and in small parties during the summer and fall when the snows were gone. Sometimes they dressed in rabbitskins and stopped to prepare acorn meal or chip arrowheads and scrapers from obsidian. While the women pounded acorns, the men fished, often saturating a likely-looking pool with the juice of the turkey mullein plant which stupified the fish and allowed them to be caught by hand. Sometimes fish nets woven from hemp were stretched across streams or the Indians pulled in fat trout on hooks made from deerbone and baited with grasshoppers.

The women carried their loads on their backs in conical baskets supported by tumplines around their foreheads. The men often knotted their goods in buckskins which were slung over their shoulders or used carrying bags made from pieces of rabbit net that had been woven from milkweed fibers.

The Paiute Indians from the Owens Valley traded salt, pinenuts, obsidian, rabbitskins, blankets, balls of tobacco, baskets, and buckskins. The Mono Lake Paiute offered pinenuts, certain fleshy caterpillars that were boiled for eating, baskets, native red and white paints, salt, and highly desirable mush made from the pupae of an insect that bred in Mono Lake.

The Western Mono, Miwok, and Yokut tribes bartered with shell money, glass beads, manzanita berries, baskets, sowberry, elderberries, and acorns.

The pinenuts came from singleleaf pines that grew on the eastern side of the Sierra Nevada. The oaks that flourished on the lower western slopes furnished the acorns — especially favored were the large bitter acorns from the black oak. Both pinenuts and acorns were staples in the diets of the Indians and there was a brisk trade across the mountains.

The pinenuts were eaten directly or often roasted in hot coals or ground into flour, but the acorns required complicated processing to remove the highly bitter tannin (which a recent analysis has put at six per cent) before they could be eaten.

The acorns were split open and the kernels taken out and spread on rocks to dry in the sun. After drying, the Indian women placed the kernels in metates or mortar-holes found in hard granite outcroppings near streams on various rancherias and along trading routes. These metates were round depressions that had been pounded into the granite by generations of Indians grinding acorns.

After the Indian women had pounded the acorns into meal with a pestle or smooth stone, the flour was sifted into baskets, with the coarser bits returned for further pounding. When enough acorns had been ground into flour it was poured into a shallow circular depression two to three feet in diameter that had been scooped in clean sand and lined with leaves.

Meanwhile hot rocks had been put into baskets to boil water that was dipped out and poured on the leaves near the center of the sand excavation. The boiling water and flour were stirred and allowed to stand. This dissolved the tannin which was drawn off by percolation through the sand. Repeated washings were required but finally the acorn flour was free of tannin. The meal was then scooped from the sand and placed in a conical basket and stirred with water. The acorn meal settled on the sides while the sand fell to the bottom. The meal was then allowed to dry thoroughly after which the unleavened loaf was broken and eaten as bread or was moistened and taken as mush.

The California Indians used many variations of this system but the essential technique was the same: the tannin was leached from the acorn flour by repeated applications of water over a sandy bottom.

A typical trading trip was recorded by J. H. Steward in *Two Paiute Autobiographies*. He took down a conversation with Sam Newland, a Paiute Indian from the Owens Valley.

"I found that the people were talking about getting salt to trade across the Sierra Nevada the next year. We went down to the salt place (a kind of brush grows on land where salt may be had) and I succeeded in making two cakes. In the spring, about June, a number of men made a trading trip. I went along with them, taking my balls of salt. I had put the salt up in balls rather than cakes because the people across the mountains like them better that way. Six of us, all men, started out late one afternoon and went the first night to tönō'vü. We always camp here the first night because there is a metate on which to grind seeds. We made short trips each day on account of our loads.

"When we reached the other side, the Indians took us in and gave us food. While we were eating with one family, someone else would come in and say, 'When you get through, come to my place,' so we would go over and eat another meal. We could talk with these people (Western Mono) in our own language, although they were a little difficult to understand.

"The next morning we began to trade. The people were always anxious to get salt and we were always ready to trade it. But they did not like the flat cakes. A man picked one up and put it aside, saying, 'This is no good, it will be used up too fast.' Then he looked at my balls and said: 'This is the kind! This has a heart and will last.' He put a red woolen blanket on a rock and said, 'Whoever owns this salt come and get it.' But my second ball of salt was too large and I could not sell it. Finally I gave it to an Indian doctor I had known. In return he gave me a long string of beads which he had worn around his neck, a spotted shirt, a pair of overalls, and a rather poor buckskin. This was

far more than I had expected to receive. The other men with me sold their salt for cloth, dresses, blankets, etc."

Between Yosemite and Mt. Whitney, five Indian trails crossed the range, linking the San Joaquin Valley on the west with the Owens Valley country on the east.

Farthest north was the Mono Lake Trail which skirted the southern cliffs above Yosemite Valley and followed the divide between the Merced and Tuolumne Rivers to Tuolumne Meadows, then went southeastward to Mono Pass and down to Mono Lake via Bloody Canyon.

The next trans-Sierra trail worked up through the forests and meadows of the northern tributaries of the San Joaquin, crossed the Middle Fork of the San Joaquin, and topped the Sierra crest at Mammoth Pass.

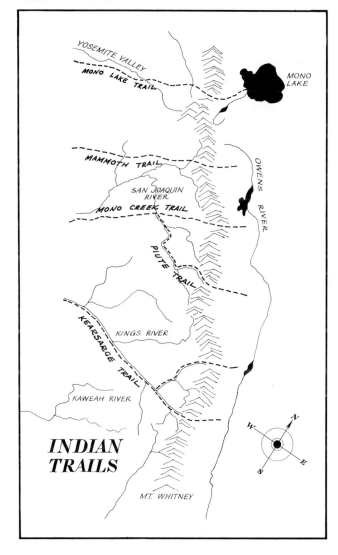

INDIAN TRAILS

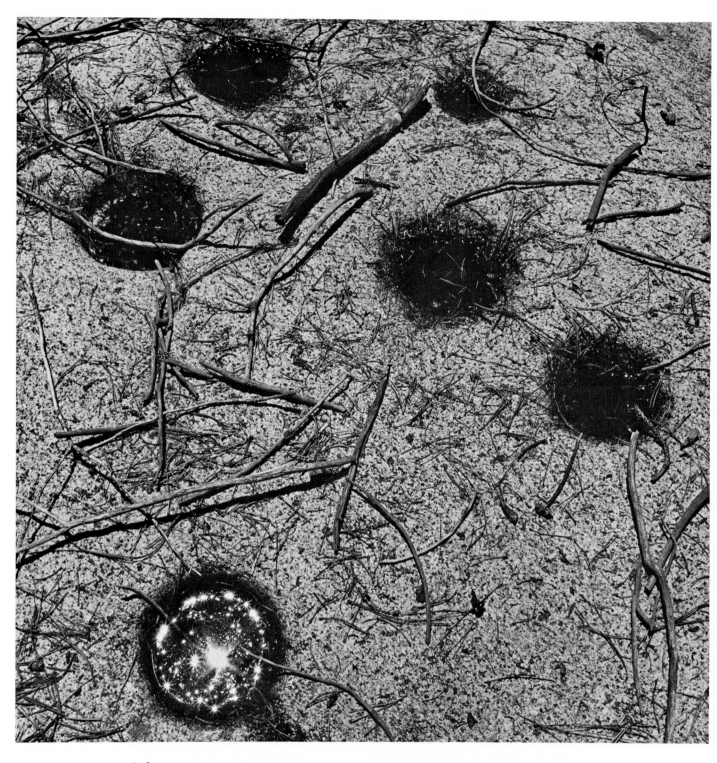

Indian metates, Little Yosemite Valley. These mortar holes in hard granite are depressions that were formed by generations of Indians pounding acorns into meal. Such metates or mortar sites are often found along old trading routes of the Indians — but always near water and sand, both of which were necessary for the complex processing of acorns into edible meal.

The Mono Creek Trail climbed the easy divide between the San Joaquin and Kings Rivers, forded the South Fork of the San Joaquin, and ascended Mono Creek to its head where it crossed the crest and dropped down Rock Creek.

The fourth route followed the South Fork of the San Joaquin River past Blaney Meadows to Piute Creek where the Indians scrambled up a rough trail to Piute Pass and descended to Owens Valley by way of Bishop Creek.

The last regular Indian crossing was at Kearsarge Pass, far to the south, where the trail scaled the divide between the Kings and Kaweah Rivers and dropped into the South Fork of the Kings. It then went east up Bubbs Creek to the crest where it plunged over Kearsarge Pass and down to Owens Valley. Another branch of this route forked north up Paradise Valley, followed Woods Creek eastward and went over the crest at Taboose Pass.

The Indians of course crossed at many other places but these routes were the principal east-west trails. In each case the object was to get across the range quickly and easily since heavy loads were often carried. In general the Indian trails followed the most accessible river drainages and kept to the most favorable ridges and canyons.

Though different tribes frequently went across the range to the home grounds of their trading opposites they sometimes met near the crest for bartering sessions. John B. Lembert, a pioneer settler who homesteaded 160 acres of land in Tuolumne Meadows in 1885, told a friend that when he first went into the meadows the Mono Indians came up in the summer months to meet the Miwok Indians from Yosemite. Both parties of Indians camped out in the middle of the meadows along the stream where the wind was blowing to get away from the mosquitos. Seventy-five to 100 Indians made up the two trading parties who with their colored blankets and deerskins and squaws and children made a tremendous sight in their encampments near the river. Many things were traded but obsidian, pinenuts, and deerskins were high on the list.[1]

Food was never scarce for Indians in the region of the Sierra Nevada except for the Paiutes who inhabited the dry Great Basin area east of the range. They had to work harder for their foodstuffs and fought to protect their vast, arid lands — especially the stands of singleleaf pines which furnished their pinenuts.

The Paiutes often had great deer drives during which the men would herd the animals into a large circle by frightening them with torches and then close in and kill them. The old men and women then cured the meat. Some cured venison was always left hanging in the mountains, *theft being impossible for anyone in need was welcome to it!*

The Paiutes had a reputation for fierceness and were cagey traders. The Yokuts feared them greatly and seldom went beyond the neutral trading ground on the eastern passes.

"If a small party of mountain Indians appeared in Yokut territory, they were generally attacked to even up old scores," wrote Indian Historian George W. Stewart. "But if the party was a large one, there was no fighting unless the invaders were the aggressors. The Yokuts attacked only small numbers unless forced to fight."[2]

Years later when a Yokut visited the Owens Valley with a group of white men and saw how easily the Paiutes got their salt he said he felt like killing them all. The clever Paiutes had always demanded high prices in goods from the tribes across the Sierra and had often compelled them to carry heavy loads long distances across the mountains for small amounts of salt.

9

YOSEMITE VALLEY TO DONOHUE PASS
The Uncertain Stream

Above Nevada Falls the John Muir Trail enters Little Yosemite Valley and follows along the north side of the Merced River for a half mile before turning abruptly north and climbing out of the valley by way of Sunrise Creek. In the photograph, taken from an airplane, we look east up the two-mile length of the valley at the young Merced River — here at 6,150 feet altitude — as it tumbles toward us on its journey to the sea.

The valley shows the rounded contours of a typical U-shaped canyon that has been gouged out by glaciers rather than the sharp V-shape of a valley cut by a stream. Glaciers came down the valley four times, twice completely overriding the canyon and its walls, and quarried out enormous masses of well-jointed rock which resulted in a short, relatively wide valley. The upper half of the valley is more narrow and steep because its rock is massive and unfractured which impeded lateral quarrying by the glaciers. This lack of cracks and joints explains the dearth of vegetation today. The smooth rocks offer no footholds for trees and bushes; all the cracked and jointed rock was carried away by the ice.

A lake once filled the entire basin of Little Yosemite Valley, measuring some two miles in length and roughly one-half-mile wide. The water lay in a hollow scooped out by the glaciers and was impounded by a rock barrier at the foot of the valley. The lake was shallow, its depth varying from 25 to 50 feet. Such a lake quickly filled up with sedimentary material carried into the valley by the river which brought soil, sand, and small rocks from above and formed a delta that gradually advanced and turned the lake to land.[1]

The meander pattern of stream flow is fascinating. A stream running in a valley whose floor is sand or gravel never flows in a straight line. At some point an obstruction to the current develops,

perhaps a rock or log or entering tributary stream. The obstruction deflects the current toward a bank which begins to erode. As the bank caves in, its sedimentary material is deposited as a bar along the same bank downstream. The new bar in turn deflects the current downstream toward the opposite bank where the process is repeated and so forth. Surprisingly enough, this can be demonstrated to perfection in just three hours in a laboratory with a model stream running in sand. The meander pattern continues with marvelous symmetry until a harder, less erodable bank is encountered which changes the pattern.[2]

Because the slope of the valley tends downstream, caving is most rapid on banks that face up the valley. This causes the whole meander structure to slowly work down the valley. Since bank material is never uniform the downstream migration moves at slightly different rates and some curves of the stream move faster than others. When a faster moving portion of a meander intersects the neck of the next downstream meander, it forms a neck cutoff which takes the main flow of the stream. The by-passed meander is called an oxbow lake and since each end is blocked with sediment, it gradually fills in. Another variation to the meander pattern occurs at times of flooding when the racing stream forms a chute cutoff by short-cutting across the meander rather than going around it.

In the overleaf photograph taken during June flooding we see a perfect oxbow lake and the remains of various by-passed meanders. The flow of the Merced River is complicated here by flooding which undermines, topples, and washes downstream hundreds of lodgepole pines which collect and dam up the river to some extent. We see that one such dam has forced much of the flow of the river back into and around the oxbow lake. The flow patterns clearly show that the most rapid water is always on the outside of each meander. The silt or stream carried material however flows more slowly and is always on the inside of the meander curve where the overladen river deposits its load in bars.

Another complicating factor in the meander flow in Little Yosemite Valley is morainal deposit. Several dozen moraines from various glacial advances and recessions lie across and along the route of the river. In the general view of the valley we see a major swing to the left, then toward us, then to the right, then toward us again. These abrupt swings are caused by small moraines lying across the valley.[3] In this case the river has cut through two moraines and then run south along a third until it reached the end of the moraine where it resumed its normal flow down the valley.

Oxbow lake, Merced River, Little Yosemite Valley.

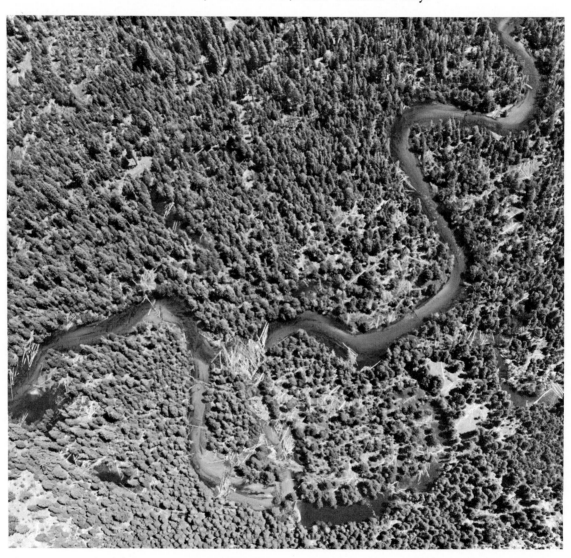

10

YOSEMITE VALLEY TO DONOHUE PASS
Sunrise High Sierra Camp

You can find food and accommodations along the 212 miles of the John Muir Trail at only two places. Both are in Yosemite and part of the loop of High Sierra camps operated by the Yosemite Park and Curry Co., the park concessioner. One camp is in Tuolumne Meadows near the junction of the Dana and Lyell forks of the young Tuolumne River. It's large and adequate, but busy and fairly noisy since it's near the Tioga Road and a good deal of summer traffic.

Sunrise Camp however, eleven miles southwest, is a long way from the road and sits on the southeast slope of Sunrise Mountain. It's wonderfully isolated and quiet with a fine view of both the southern hook of Long Meadow and south across high rocky moraines to the canyon of the Merced River and beyond to the spurs and ridges which climb to Mt. Clark. The camp — at 9,400 feet — is just above the meadow proper and its tents and buildings are so well hidden among the trees and boulders that you can easily miss it.

Sunrise is a tiny camp, with a capacity for 34 guests, and open only during the eight weeks of July and August. Because of its small size you must have reservations, best gotten months in advance but sometimes obtainable at the last minute. Guests sleep on beds with springs and mattresses in large floored tents. Each tent takes from four to six and has a wood stove and lanterns. There are modern toilets in the washhouse which surprisingly also has hot showers (the water is warmed by circulating it through copper coils inside sun-heated glass-topped boxes after which it is finally heated by butane). The camp is run by a manager and his wife who doubles as cook plus four college-age helpers.

The meals at Sunrise are superb, considering the location. Breakfast and supper are ample and appetizing by any standards. Box lunches are supplied for the noon meal, since everyone is either going or coming or out somewhere.

Sunrise was built to fulfill a dream of Mary Curry Tresidder, head of the Yosemite Park and Curry Co., who first camped on the site in 1934. She long thought of a small camp above a beautiful mountain meadow and when the Park Service gave its permission for a new camp in 1960, Mrs. Tresidder paid for one-half its cost from her own funds. The charges at Sunrise are quite modest considering that everything is first-class and has been brought in on mules. The company loses about $5,000 a year on its six High Sierra camps but feels they should be continued. In no other place in the United States can you find such an easy and pleasant introduction to the back country.

A person stopping at one of the camps immediately senses a receptive and generally happy feeling. The people who run the camps are especially chosen because they like the high mountains and can appreciate the moods and feelings of their arriving guests. The staff is of course expert at setting a good table and must occasionally be clever and ingenious when something breaks down or fails to arrive. But the main thing is not a fancy *soufflé au Grand Marnier* or *steak au poivre*, but a friendly greeting when you come in happily exhausted from a long day on the trail.

Long Meadow and Mt. Clark

Aerial view northeast across Sunrise Mountain toward Cathedral Pass.

11

YOSEMITE VALLEY TO DONOHUE PASS
Dome Country

If you hire an airplane and fly low over the high country of Yosemite you will see an area of enormous domes of stone surmounted here and there by jagged peaks. Between the masses of granite are green meadows circled by sparse forests of lodgepole pines which gradually thin out to nothing as they climb up the sides of the increasingly smooth domes.

The agent responsible for much of this landscape was ice. Twice the whole area was overrun by glaciers which ground off all the jointed and fractured rock they could reach. Everything with cracks or seams that could be torn open was gouged into, ripped off, and pushed away toward the lowlands. Whenever the abrading glaciers met more resistant, unfractured rock however, the ice was forced over and around the harder strata, leaving rough domes whose size and form depended on the toughness and massiveness of the rock. Sometimes the glacial scouring left gently rising domes; often the projections were massive and thumblike — big enough and steep enough to make today's viewers lose all sense of scale. Fairview Dome for example, the thrusting, rounded cone just left of Cathedral Peak in the top part of the photograph, shoots up 1,341 feet above a survey marker only one-half mile away.

The ice was deep; its extent enormous. The Merced glacier of the Wisconsin ice age measured 70 square miles and in this high country swept over everything except the tallest peaks which today largely retain the sharp spires and points of preglacial times. To the northeast, in the distance, the Tuolumne glacier was even larger — 140 square miles of grinding ice that covered Tuolumne Meadows to a depth of 2,200 feet.[1]

From our airplane we can see dozens of small and large domes that were roughed into shape by the ice. We also can see the peaks and ridges that were above the glaciers — the island tops in vast oceans of ice. Looking at the photograph we face northeast and see the serrated tops of Cathedral and Echo Peaks (center, middleground), the Cockscomb, and Unicorn Peak. In front of Cathedral Peak is the roughcast battlement of Columbia Finger; in the center foreground is the ridge of Sunrise Mountain, running diagonally from left to right paralleling the green swale of Long Meadow directly behind. In front of Sunrise Mountain where Long Meadow hooks to our left is Sunrise High Sierra Camp. The route of the John Muir Trail runs from the bottom left corner of the photograph and follows up Long Meadow to the right of Sunrise Mountain. It then swings to the right around Columbia Finger, crosses Cathedral Pass in the shadow of its namesake, and continues northeastward to Tuolumne Meadows, just visible in the right background.

If you climb up on the higher, rougher spires you won't find glacial scratches or traces of moraines. You will find instead — along with hard climbing — large and small squarish blocks of frost-fractured granite often with weathered surfaces. A little lower down you encounter the ice line where the appearance of the spires changes abruptly. Here where the glacial ice flowed, the mountains have a sculptured look since the work of the ice was largely erosional. You will see plenty of glacial scratch marks and polish which indicate the direction of the ice and sometimes you will have to climb over tumbled heaps of ice-transported boulders and rocks (this explains how you occasionally see the paradox of a huge boulder perched on top of a ridge or dome or other unlikely place. The boulder — along with a mass of smaller rocks and soil — was carried by the ice. The smaller materials have disappeared, leaving only the solitary, amazingly located boulder).

The other significant factor in the formation of domes is a process called exfoliation, defined by Geologist François Matthes as "the casting off of successive curving shells or scales from their exposed surfaces." Every granite dome has many such curving shells, arranged about one another like the layers of an onion. The outer layers slowly break up and fall off. These exfoliated shells vary in thickness from six inches up to an exceptional 100 feet, though six to ten feet are more ordinary. The exact causes for exfoliation are uncertain but expansion from hydration and hydrolysis, internal stresses and pressures, and heating by the sun are important. The process is slow, incredibly slow.

According to Matthes, exfoliation requires 2,000 *centuries* to moderately round off an angular edge by removing perhaps ten feet.[2]

Because it's so easy to survey the area in a few seconds from an airplane it's hard to realize how slowly the landscape below has developed. The flows of ice came and vanished, roughing out the domes and by-passing a few higher spires. Frost, running water, exfoliation, and the actions of plants have all been at work for millions of summers and winters, changing, modifying, and shaping the land into the wonderful mountain landscape of today.

12

YOSEMITE VALLEY TO DONOHUE PASS
The Ghost Forests

Between Cathedral Pass and Tuolumne Meadows are thousands of acres of lodgepole pines, the most common tree of the high mountains and one that runs along the timberline country for hundreds of miles. Lumbermen scoff at the lodgepole when comparing it with Douglas fir or ponderosa pine, but the mountaineer treats the often scraggly, scaly-barked lodgepole with affection for it grows in places he likes and is usually the tree that provides the wood for his campfire and protection for his camp at night.

In the drainages of the upper Tuolumne River however, the lodgepole forests have been plagued periodically by a pink-colored caterpillar called the lodgepole needle miner. This insect is about as thick as thin pencil lead and is a quarter of an inch long. By himself he's harmless, but in company with millions of his fellows he can cause quite a commotion. Each larva of the needle miner — which becomes a tiny greyish moth with a wing-

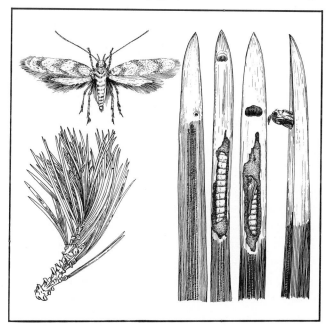

spread of a quarter of an inch when mature — eats, or rather mines out, from three to five pine needles, hollowing out the leaves and causing them to turn yellow and die, giving the forest a brownish tinge instead of its natural green.

The life cycle of a needle miner lasts two years. Whether by chance or unknown design the adults in this region hatch during July and August of odd-numbered years. Since the insects eat more needles as they grow, an infested forest is always browner in the spring of odd-numbered years. During the first year the activity of the insects is less and the trees can recover to some extent. But in places where the infestation is heavy the trees die; four generations usually cause enough defoliation to kill a tree. If you cut through a branch of an infested tree and inspect the annual rings you will see that the annual growth has gotten less and less as the insects have eaten the leaves.

Some entomologists and the National Park Service consider the needle miner to be a harmful and destructive pest. Other entomologists and observers believe the insect to be important in keeping lodgepole pine forests vigorous and healthy by thinning adult trees. Often the mountain pine beetle attacks trees weakened by the needle miner although experts are unsure of the relationship. In any case the latest Yosemite needle miner expansion commenced in 1945, increased to nearly 50,000 acres by 1955, and grew to 89,000 acres by 1963, leaving thousands of dead trees behind.[1] The needle miner is not new; a combination of the needle miner and pine beetle has swept the same forests at least twice before in this century and in many places ghost forests of lodgepole snags still stand, though vigorous young lodgepoles surround almost every bleaching trunk.

As long ago as 1869 John Muir saw "large patches and strips of dead bleached spars, the

Healthy lodgepole foliage.

Defoliated lodgepole.

ground beneath them covered with a young even growth," when he explored north of Soda Springs.[2] He was puzzled because all the trees seemed to be the same age. He guessed at fire as the cause. It may have been, but in 1894, after an expedition to northern Yosemite, First Lieutenant N. F. Mc-Clure of the Fifth Cavalry wrote: "The march had taken us through another of the great wonders of the region, namely, the 'Dead Forest.' . . . the cañon is very broad, and covered with tamarack trees, almost every one of which is dead. The reason for this unusual freak of nature I do not know."[3]

In 1903 a ranger noticed "white flies that seem to be killing the pine trees."[4] Ten years later the annual report of the Superintendent of Yosemite Park noted: "Messrs. Miller and Sullivan, entimologists, Agricultural Department, were engaged during the late spring and summer months in investigating the life history of the pests (needle borer and bark beetle) which are destroying the tamarack pine. . . . A ranger has been instructed by these gentlemen and will continue the work begun by them in the effort to rid the park of the pest and save the timber. The ranger reports that 1,335 trees in the general vicinity of Lake Tenaya and McGee Lake Trail have been cut down and 1,250 of them burned in the efforts to conquer the in-

festation. This procedure must be continued until the bugs are destroyed, lest all of the lodgepole in the whole park be destroyed, after which the other and more valuable species will be attacked."[5]

Investigators have shown that the present epidemic has followed a pattern similar to two previous outbreaks, one from 1910 to 1922, and a second from 1933 to 1940.[6] Both attacks, perhaps in combination with the mountain pine beetle, caused extensive ghost forests of dead trees, many of which are still standing among the new lodgepole forests more recently infested.

When I visited Yosemite in 1963 and talked to Park Superintendent John C. Preston, he told me of his concern.

"Today, besides the danger to other trees in Yosemite and adjacent national forests, we are gravely worried about the loss of forest recreational areas," said Preston. "Thousands of visitors go to Tuolumne Meadows during the summer. In the campgrounds and picnic sites the shading pine canopy is an important part of the natural scene. Loss of the trees results not only in the destruction of aesthetic values around lakes, along trails, and on the mountain slopes, but makes such expensive developments as campgrounds, picnic tables, water lines, rangers' cabins, and toilets relatively useless.

64

Ghost forest of lodgepole snags near Tenaya Lake. Note the vigorous growth of young trees.

Scientists at Cathedral Creek checking the toxicity of spraying by counting the number of dead needle miners on a calibrated drop cloth.

Entomologists in Tuolumne Meadows evaluating needle miner populations.

"Who wants to camp in a ghost forest with dead pine needles showering down on you?" said Preston.

The most obvious step was to call in entomologists. Since little was known about the needle miner, scientists of the U. S. Forest Service, working under the supervision of the National Park Service, began to study the insect. Spraying was a possible solution but what to spray and how to spray were difficult problems. In 1948 the infestation was small and it was hoped that prompt spraying with DDT, which had been 95 per cent effective against the spruce bud worm in Idaho, would end the trouble.

"Then our problems really started," recalled the late Yosemite Forester Emil Ernst. "First we planned to use a helicopter. We hoped that its hovering ability and slow flying speed would be ideal for the terrain. But in the thin air above Tuolumne Meadows the poor helicopter almost fanned itself to death without a payload. The pilot had to throw off everything but his shoes to get aloft. It was a complete failure.[7]

In August 1949, an experienced cropduster from Fresno was hired to spray 1,000 acres in Tenaya Gap. The area was a long basin at 9,000 feet altitude between high granite cliffs swept by tricky air currents. At that altitude the power of the Stearman Biplane's engine was greatly reduced. The pilot made two low passes over the trees and landed, "I quit," he said. "Too hazardous. Besides I have a wife and kids. . . ."

In 1953, $14,000 was budgeted for a converted B-18 two-engine bomber to spray 11,000 acres with DDT. Indicator drop cards were placed among the trees to record the effectiveness of the spray coverage which was to be timed with the hatching of the needle miner larvae. On September 9th the entomologists reported that 90 per cent of the eggs had hatched. The word was relayed to the Deadman Summit Airstrip and the B-18 took to the air, headed for Tuolumne Meadows, and began spraying. Some 11,000 gallons of DDT were dropped on 19 flights.

Down in the forest the indicator drop cards showed excellent deposits of spray. Everyone was jubilant, but the needle miners were probably the happiest because the DDT did nothing.

"Our later studies showed that DDT was the poorest insecticide we could have used," said U. S. Forest Service Entomologist George Struble. "The spray job was operationally successful but an entomological flop."

In 1954, the mountain pine beetle populations increased, killing many trees weakened by the needle miner. Thousands of lodgepoles showed the characteristic signatures of pine beetles under the bark. An $18,000 beetle control project, supplied by an air drop, was attempted in Conness Basin, north of Tuolumne Meadows, scene of the heaviest needle miner concentrations. About 1700 trees were treated by felling and burning. A later survey showed an additional 3,945 beetle-infested trees in the area.[8]

A summer field camp staffed by four entomologists was established in Tuolumne Meadows in 1955 to conduct an intensive study of the insect and to look into various control methods. Because the needle miner has a 24-month life cycle, research was charted for five generations or ten years — to 1965. Basic biological studies included sampling counts of the egg, larval, pupal, and adult stages to record each growth level to help plot the degree and course of the insect population.

Scientists at the University of California began to study native enemies of the needle miner — control organisms such as parasitic wasps and woolly aphids — to find ways to increase the effectiveness of the natural biological controls. However one quick control possibility, outside of natural enemies of the needle miner, was new and powerful insecticides which were being used elsewhere by the Forest Service. Organic phosphates such as malathion were potent killers. "Just a flick of the sprayer and every insect in the area exposed to the dilute poison was killed," reported Entomologist George Struble after a test in Tuolumne Meadows. "We put cloths under sprayed trees to keep track of dead moths and collected up to 500 adult needle miners from a single branch.

"But testing insecticides is far more complex than spraying a few trees," said Struble. "We had to find out how long the sprays lasted, the correct dilution, how they affected the trees, and what happened to fish and wildlife."

Coupled with these unknown factors was the question of the effect of such chemicals on water —

Helicopters reloading with insecticide, Tuolumne Meadows.

especially since all back country campers in the High Sierra drink from streams.

In 1957, test plots were sprayed from a Bell helicopter. By 1959, park officials had enough confidence in the control methods developed by the Forest Service entomologists to spend $100,000 for a full scale application.[9] The insecticide was to be one gallon of malathion diluted with ten gallons of Diesel oil per acre. More powerful helicopters were available — though they cost $300 an hour — and 3400 acres of lodgepoles were sprayed in the recreational areas around Tuolumne Meadows. This time millions of needle miners were killed — 75 per cent according to the Forest Service. During the summer of 1961, 4800 acres were sprayed, and in 1963, an additional 4800 acres were covered. To combat the secondary problem of the mountain pine beetle, a water emulsion of ethylene dibromide was sprayed from a lightweight motor-driven pressure rig on the ground to a trunk height of 40 feet.

Biologists investigated the effects of the malathion spraying in 1963. A 21-day bird count showed populations down ten per cent in sprayed areas. During four weeks of observation no differences were noted between control and test groups of rodents and birds exposed to aerial applications of malathion and fed food similarly exposed. The helicopter pilots had been instructed not to spray near streams; careful checks showed no water

contamination. There was a small loss of fish in pools, perhaps from the Diesel oil which was washed down by rain and killed small water insects on which the trout existed.

Chicken eggs at various stages of incubation were exposed at different tree heights and on the ground. The eggs "suffered striking mortality." Most embryos died and exhibited massive hemorrhages suggestive of anoxia while other chicks were deformed upon hatching. "Results . . . suggest that spraying could influence bird nesting success," noted the U. S. Fish and Wildlife Service.[10]

The story would be simple if we could stop after reporting control of pests by insecticides, say that the lodgepole forests in the area are healthy and thriving, and pass off the reported small wildlife losses as an unpleasant necessity. Unfortunately the story is more complicated.

Yosemite is part of the National Park System which was established by Congress in 1916. Part of the agency's task by law is "to conserve the scenery and the natural and historic objects and the wild life therein and to provide for the enjoyment of the same in such manner and by such means as will leave them unimpaired for the enjoyment of future generations." Ideally this means leaving the park as the first Europeans saw it, admittedly an impossible task but not an impractical goal.

Under the Forest Pest Control Act, U. S. Forest Service entomologists make recommendations to National Park officials about insect problems in national parks. The Forest Service however is charged by law with timber production, watershed protection, grazing rights, mining supervision, and visitor use of national forests, an entirely different set of ground rules. When insects infest trees in national forests the responsibility of its entomologists is to kill or control the insects to protect potential lumber. The Forest Service tends to draw from the great fund of agricultural pest control knowledge. The Park Service, however, is charged to protect the natural scene, all of it, and the insecticide programs of food and fiber technologists, looking for quick solutions to pest problems, seem hardly adaptable to national parks. Perhaps the National Park Service should hire its own entomologists who could work on such biological controls as encouraging natural enemies or introducing a specific disease to reduce an unwanted insect population.

Both the needle miner and lodgepole pine are native to Yosemite; each has existed in the other's environment for perhaps thousands of years. The needle miner caterpillars attack older trees, kill certain of them, and open the forest which in turn encourages the growth of younger lodgepoles. If you walk through the forests under question you will see that a vigorous growth of young trees surrounds each dead snag. If you make measurements over several years you will find that the lodgepole is fast growing and spreads quickly, often in thick groves. Unfortunately man has chosen to build a road and establish campgrounds where the needle miner is at work.

The lodgepole and needle miner are both parts of a complex ecological relationship which means that they cannot succeed or multiply beyond a point without encountering natural controls that put them back in their proper place. Young trees on the edge of grassland advance on the grass during wet years; when the drought returns, the larger, closer-to-the-surface root systems of the grass take the moisture and the trees die out; the boundary is stabilized.[11]

A program to shoot mountain lions and coyotes removes the natural control on a deer herd which increases until it overbrowses its range which in turn deteriorates and causes the excess deer to starve until the herd once more fits its range. [12] A forest is protected from small periodic ground fires — usually set by lightning—until dense thickets of undergrowth encircle the larger trees, changing growth patterns and species, and offering ample fuel for catastrophic wildfire, which once started will take out the whole forest.[13]

Entomologists have stated that parasites are the most important natural enemies of the needle miner. One researcher found a 42 per cent drop in needle miner hatchings between 1957 and 1959 and suggested that its natural enemies were increasing.[14] Another authority, Dr. Alan D. Telford, felt confident that these natural enemies, which included some 40 varieties of parasitic wasps and many birds, were growing in number and force and might well control the needle miner. Yet an improperly timed spray was more detrimental to the parasite population than to the needle miner. The malathion oil spray rather than helping the natural control factor, "killed the principal parasites," he noted in one study.[15] Violent disagreements with Forest Service entomologists led to his dismissal from the project.

As we have seen, the needle miner has occurred periodically for a very long time; obviously, natural biological controls exist. If poisons spread by man kill or interfere with these natural enemies of the needle miner, the occasional epidemics may become permanent, requiring spraying every other year indefinitely at a high cost in dollars and ultimately producing drastically weakened forests. Biological controls, where nature *assists* man, are infinitely cheaper.

"In a forest where conditions are conducive to needle miner outbreak, the outbreak occurs, waxes, eliminates conditions which stimulated the outbreak and subsequently wanes," wrote Dr. Telford in March, 1964. "If an outbreak is suppressed by an insecticide the conditions conducive to outbreak remain and can increase outbreak potential."[16]

Biological controls need not be microscopic. Insectivorous birds eat caterpillars in high numbers. More than 275 caterpillars have been removed from the stomach of a single chickadee.[17] The 1963 study by the U. S. Fish and Wildlife Service reported: "About 25 birds of four species were collected for stomach analysis. Examinations revealed that the siskins and finches specifically were crammed full of needle miner larvae. This indicates that they are probably the most effective natural control in the area at this time." Unfortunately, as we have seen, the same study contained a test of simulated bird nesting in which chicken eggs were sprayed with malathion and "suffered striking mortality."[18] An earlier study by the same agency showed that "bird populations were reduced by one-half, six weeks after applications; evidently birds moved away from treated areas in reaction to decreased food supplies."[19]

The problem in Yosemite boils down to how to protect the natural scene. A good many competent scientists (and some people within the Park Service itself) feel that all spraying should be stopped. They suggest that the money spent on needle miner control could have built a good many campgrounds elsewhere. The argument that only 5.4 per cent of the infested area is being sprayed can be countered, say opponents of spraying, by pointing out that this percentage represents places visitors should be shown natural scenes, not experimental forests. One of the attractions of Hawaii National Park, for example, is a picturesque forest killed by volcanic ash. The Leopold Report of 1963, requested and approved by the Secretary of the Interior stated: "We wish to raise a serious question about the mass application of insecticides in the control of forest insects. Such applications may (or may not) be justified in commercial timber stands, but in a national park ecologic impact can have unanticipated effects on the biotic community that might defeat the over-all management objective."[20]

Most conservationists believe that national parks should be places where man can see nature at work undisturbed. Events such as insect attacks and forest dieback and regrowth are significant parts of the complicated growth, the *very building process* of forests. They are more than showcases of natural forces; they are the life force at work, the self-same force that built man unassisted by man.

"The lodgepole pine forms the base of an intricate wildlife pyramid," one expert wrote recently. "In addition to bark beetles and needle miners, wood-boring beetles, ants, woodpeckers, chickadees, chipmunks, hawks, and owls are part of the pyramid. All are dependent upon a continual crop of dead and dying lodgepole pine."[21]

"I agree that there are conditions where nature should have its way," Yosemite Park Superintendent Preston told me. "In remote areas where there are few people and there is less fire hazard from dead snags there certainly is no objection to leaving things as nature dictates. It is not our objective to totally eradicate the needle miner or even to control it over its entire range. We know the needle miner is not new in the forests; perhaps it is as old as the lodgepole itself.

"But in the Tuolumne Meadows area where thousands of people go for recreation we believe that needle miner destruction is harmful. We believe we have an obligation to keep the area as usable as possible. Undertaking spraying was a difficult decision.

"The lodgepole needle miner project in Yosemite is the first successful control of this insect," added Preston. "In 1963 we sprayed 4,800 acres out of 89,000 or about 5.4 per cent. Our control program cost only $12.85 per acre, which is considered quite reasonable. Our objective has been to hold a green belt along roads, major trails, and developed areas so that people can continue to enjoy this part of the High Sierra."

But in many of the thousands of acres around Tuolumne Meadows any discussion of the needle miner has become somewhat academic. Though park administrators believe they have found an effective insecticide and have learned how to apply it to forest areas, it is still too late to save the hundreds of thousands of lodgepoles that have already died from this cause — if indeed the individual trees needed to be saved.

The old ghost forests stand and thousands of acres of new ghost forests are in the making. Chances are, this is about how the score has read through the ages — ages that have seen the lodgepole overpopulation thinned out by the needle miner, and in turn the needle miner overpopulation thinned out by parasites and birds — with always enough for posterity to continue. Nature takes and nature gives; life goes on.

Cathedral Pass

Aerial view northeast across Cathedral Pass (center foreground). Cathedral Peak and Upper Cathedral Lake at left. Unicorn Peak and Budd Lake at right in middleground. Mt. Dana (left) and Mt. Gibbs on the skyline.

13

YOSEMITE VALLEY TO DONOHUE PASS
Deer, Tuolumne Meadows

The deer herds of Yosemite total 20,000 animals and every year — on the average — 4,000 of them starve to death. Their story is complicated, morosely fascinating, and a superb example of the meaning of ecology — that science of living things, their relationships to each other, and to their environment. In the case of Sierra deer, man's meddling is responsible for grievous problems — or at least partly responsible. But let the story speak . . .

The principal deer of the Sierra Nevada is the California mule deer. An average buck is 5 feet 7 inches long, stands 40 inches high at the shoulder, and weighs up to 170 pounds. Does are a bit smaller. Both have large mule-like ears, 8 to 9 inches long and four inches wide. The tail is white, slender, and black-tipped, or more rarely black striped. The coats of the adults are reddish-brown in summer and grayish-brown in winter. The rump, throat, and belly are whitish.[1]

The bone-like antlers are found only on the male who grows spike horns his second summer. The antlers are shed each January or February; by the end of April the new horns are one inch high, 7 to 10 inches high by June 30, and fully grown by early August. Each year the new antlers grow longer and tend to branch more and more. The developing antlers are covered with highly vascularized soft skin called velvet which grows along with the horns. When the antler growth is finished the velvet dries up and is rubbed off — usually by mid-September — leaving the familiar bony horns.[2]

During November the necks of the bucks begin to swell with the ruts which last through December. Some of the males fight, and ground areas are often pawed where bucks have been threatening one another. There are often two does to each buck though the ratio varies.

The young are born during June and July after a seven-month period of gestation. They are usually dropped in wet meadows where there is plenty of nutritious green food for the does and ample cover for the new arrivals. One fawn is usually born but twins are quite common. The young deer, camouflaged to some extent by white spots on their reddish-brown coats, are too weak to run much at first and crouch quietly among corn lilies or thickets of aspens or willows to avoid detection by predators or people, often hiding themselves remarkably well. Fawns are always found near surface water and after weaning tend to feed on succulent vegetation rather than dry browse.

There are a few records of golden eagles and wildcats taking fawns but such predation is rare. Black bears and coyotes kill more deer, especially the very young, the old, the weak, and cripples. Coyotes often do well when heavy snow slows the deer in winter but under normal conditions a healthy adult can easily outrun a bear or coyote.

Since 1907, the State of California has paid a bounty for the killing of mountain lions (male $50; female $60) and up to 1963, 12,461 lions were shot by private and state-hired hunters. The original reason for putting a high bounty on mountain lions was to allow deer to increase after enormous and uncontrolled hunting in the early days of the state had devastated the herds. Tens of thousands of deer were slaughtered for their hides, to feed mining camps, and to make jerky.[3] But that was long ago and since the deer herds are now large again, there is no longer the slightest necessity to shoot these magnificent lions which are rarely seen, never bother man, and in fact shun human activities completely. Biologists estimate that an individual lion kills about 36 deer a year which helps keep deer herds trim and healthy, certainly a good reason to encourage the species which in any case will never be very prevalent. Predation by lions is one factor that helps fit a deer herd to its range and assists therefore in maintining good rangelands in parks and forests. The state discontinued paying lion bounties in 1963 but the animals are still classified as predators and regrettably may be shot at any time. (Bounties are still paid by some counties.) Many naturalists, biologists, and people with knowledge of deer management hope the state action will be broadened to outlaw lion shooting entirely.

From 1947 to 1949, four biologists — including Dr. A. Starker Leopold — conducted an exhaustive study of the Jawbone herd, a typical western slope Sierra deer herd. One of the most surprising findings was that deer have definite winter and summer feeding grounds to which they return year after year. Each adult deer knows precisely where it is going and the animals move on exact, clearly marked, and easily followed routes during their spring and fall migrations, living at 1,500 to 4,000 feet altitude during the winter, and summering on the edges of forests at 6,000 to 7,500 feet and higher. Though groups of deer often travel together, each seems individually motivated and starts downward at the onset of snow and cold in October or early November, and upward with the appearance of new green growth in the spring, following perhaps 1,000 feet below the slowly retreating snow line.

The feeding ground of each deer must contain bedding sites—often in places where a deer can see about—adequate water, and of course, food. Contrary to popular belief a deer does not wander randomly over wide areas in the summer but sticks to a small range with a diameter of 1/2 to 3/4 of a mile. The winter home of a Sierra deer is even more restricted. Careful study, observations, and trapping of marked deer has shown that an average buck winters on an area 760 yards in diameter; a doe lives in a circle which measures only 320 yards in diameter. In other words, though migrating from 5 to 40 miles, the deer remain sedentary in their summer range and even more so in their restricted winter sites. The herd in the study for example, consisted of about 6,000 animals whose summer range was 267 square miles but whose winter grounds totaled only 37 square miles. Almost half a deer's life is spent on winter range

that measures but one-seventh of his summer grounds.

While in their home ranges the deer often play hide-and-seek with hunters who swear there's not a deer within miles when half a dozen animals are sometimes within the radius of their flickering campfires. Experience is important in deer sighting. In extensive interviews, hunters reported seeing 3.5 deer per day while hunting in a certain place. An experienced observer working in the same area at the same time classified 60 deer in two days.

Since deer live in small areas most of the year, their feeding habits drastically influence plant growth. A large herd tends to consume most or all of the available plant growth. When this is gone they are forced to less desirable species. If the small winter range becomes too overcrowded and heavy snow falls, deer begin to starve by the hundreds because the remaining plants with marginal nutrition are buried or partially buried and the animals waste more energy than they gain in digging them out. Unfortunately deer are reluctant to leave their home grounds and doggedly stay on; not until the old deer and fawns are dead do the survivors seek lower altitudes.

When the deer arrive at their winter feeding grounds they commence eating the new, tender twigs of the best browse plants. First they take various forms of ceanothus—buck brush and deer brush, the mainstay of the California mule deer—and then western mountain mahogany. These choice plants are nutritious and high in protein. Western mountain mahogany for example has a crude protein content of 14 per cent in October (compared with 14.7 per cent for good alfalfa). But if a herd is too large all the best twigs are soon gone. Further back from the tips the branches have less nutritive value and as winter progresses the protein content diminishes. By February and March the weaker animals—at least 20 to 35 per cent of the herd—are on the edge of starvation. Competition for food becomes keen. Fawns and old deer begin to weaken. During mild winters the loss may be 5 per cent; in a severe winter 40 per cent may perish. The average loss by starvation is 20 per cent or more.[4]

As long as the diet of a deer includes roughly half buck brush (about 8.5 per cent protein in December-February) and not over half inferior browse species (5 to 8 per cent protein) it will survive. But when the protein level of the 2½ pounds of browse a deer eats each day drops below 7 to 8 per cent the critical point is passed and the deer dies. This explains the puzzle of why the stomachs of deer that have starved to death are usually found stuffed with browse. They have been forced to eat second-class plant material incapable of sustaining life.

Deer brush on winter ranges can stand only a certain amount of eating. Botanists have found that browsing which removes more than 60 per cent of new growth tends to kill a plant. In the Jawbone herd study, the animals consumed 59 to 67 per cent of the new growth of sampled plants and clearly showed that an over-large herd will ultimately severely damage—perhaps irretrievably —its winter range, bringing about even greater catastrophe to the herd the following winter when there will be still less food.

In a 1940 study in Kings Canyon National Park, bitter cherry inside a fenced plot grew vigorously with new sprouts 5 to 6 feet high; snow-brush was 4 feet tall and showed healthy growth. Outside the fenced plot, however, deer had browsed a large part of the forest to death.[5]

When lower branches of plants are gone, deer often stand on their hind legs with their front feet placed on a trunk or limb to reach up for palatable branches. A severely overbrowsed forest soon assumes the look of a clipped park. Photographs of the Kaibab Forest in Arizona where almost total predator control was practiced for many years show an incredible scene; as far as the eye can see all brush, flowers, tree seedlings, and forest understory are gone and the trees have been eaten bare of branches to the maximum height the deer could stretch to, making the undersides of the trees resemble a sort of vast upside-down clipped hedge— for miles and miles!

Another factor in browse is fire. Historically, small lightning-set fires have burned through forest areas, clearing out old brush to make room for new sprouting the following spring. In the Sierra, Indians evidently set fires for centuries to encourage deer which thrived on the new, easy-to-reach brush. With a policy of rigid fire control in national parks and forests however, deer brush in many places has grown far above the reach of the animals, besides stockpiling enormous quantities of fuel potential to catastrophic and all-destroying wildfire.

The problem of deer and range may be illustrated by the following: Suppose 10 milk cows live on 10 acres of pasture. The cows are healthy and give good milk and the pasture is in excellent condition and looks fresh and green each spring. Now if we put 20 cows on the same pasture they will all survive but not look as healthy. The milk quality will decline somewhat and the meadow will look poorer. If we put 40 cows on the same 10 acres there will be so much competition for grass that some of the animals will lose out and sicken and perhaps die. The quantity and quality of milk will seriously decline and the meadow will approach ruin with gullies and washouts beginning in places where the grass has been cropped to extinction. Eventually there will be no cows and no meadow.

Hunting is not allowed in Yosemite National Park of course but immediately over the boundaries the hunters wait with loaded rifles every autumn. Unfortunately for the mountain rangelands, few deer are killed in spite of large numbers of hunters because hunting is restricted to adult bucks. Other reasons for poor shooting are heavy ground cover, rough topography, and a general lack of skill among hunters, most of whom, too lazy to go to the back country, remain near their cars close to roads and main camps instead of going out where the deer haven't been scared by gunfire. Another factor contributing to poor hunting—roughly one man in 20 gets a deer—is the practice of setting deer seasons by custom rather than with knowledge of deer migration habits. In the Yosemite area, the hunting season is over before most deer have left the park. If the season were adjusted to actual migrations a few weeks later, the buck kill might be increased 30 per cent.

The study of the Jawbone herd showed that out of a population which averaged 6,000 deer, hunters took only 400 bucks or about 7 per cent. The normal rate of increase of the herd was 32 per cent but since the limiting factor was the small winter range, any excess deer above the 6,000 starved. In other words if hunting practices were to follow deer management suggestions of a greatly liberalized hunting policy, far more deer might be

taken—at least three times as many—which would vastly improve the winter range, help the summer range, and give more hunters a deer. This means of course shooting does as well as bucks. Such a policy would substitute increased hunting for starvation as a population control and help keep the national parks and forests in the Sierra Nevada in better condition.

Wildlife research has shown that heavily hunted animals always reproduce faster. This has been amply documented, one notable example being a large deer herd in Stanislaus National Forest that was accidentally infected with hoof and mouth disease from cattle in 1924. Authorities decided to destroy the herd which was estimated at 10,000 animals. The use of poisoned salt and federal hunters accounted for an official kill of 22,214 deer (some estimates of the total kill ran to 40,000) before the dreaded disease was controlled. The large number of deer killed surprised everyone. All the deer weren't killed of course and in less than ten years the herd was back up to large numbers, demonstrating that deer can withstand tre-

mendous hunting pressure without keeping their numbers down for long.

The suggestion has often been made that excess deer be fed artificially. Well-meaning groups of sportsmen have fed alfalfa and various supplements to deer but besides being expensive, it just doesn't work—the deer die anyway.

The above photograph of deer in Tuolumne Meadows was taken in July, five months after they started their upward migrations. Deer often feed on forbes, weeds, and new grasses in addition to brush, but after five months of following spring growth the animals should be fat and healthy, not thin with rough coats and their ribs and backbones showing as they do in the picture.

The Jawbone herd we have been talking about lives just northwest of Yosemite but the life habits of the six deer herds of Yosemite are similar. One Yosemite herd, the East Side herd, that partially summers on Tuolumne Meadows, is composed of Inyo mule deer, a closely related sub-species that winters north of Mono Lake and whose life is closely tied to sagebrush instead of ceanothus.

Alpine Willow

In moist meadows at altitudes of 9,000 to 11,500 feet we find the alpine willow (*Salix petrophila*), a tiny plant that scarcely fills the palm of your hand. By definition the alpine willow is a tree (a perennial woody plant having a single main axis) but it seems more an herb or a midget shrub, for its stem is creeping and its erect branches reach up only two to four inches.

You often find hundreds of these willows crowded together in Lilliputian forests in the lee of sheltering rocks along rivulets and young streams in scraps of high meadow. If you lie on your stomach to examine them (a process in which you're sure to get wet from the spongy meadow) the view seems almost like that from an airplane winging low over a grove of Douglas firs or redwoods.

The seeds of this willow mature on the ends of the scaly spikes in September and are tiny bits of white or brown fluff, beautiful when backlighted. A mass of alpine willow then seems soft and silky, perfect pillow stuffing, a greyish carpet whose every fiber is crowned with a feathery ball of shimmering silver.

Girl, Lyell Fork
of the Tuolumne River

Ah tranquility! What a lovely moment. A time of delight that can't be measured nor weighed, but only felt. . . . To sit quietly and to paddle your feet in a stream. To think of nothing in particular. . . . To slip into a world of reverie, of dreams, of watching grasses idly waving in the water, a trout nibbling at something in the current, a bird gliding past.

You lie back on the bank and watch wisps of clouds form and disappear and form again. The sun is warm and you roll over on your stomach and support yourself on your elbows and examine the grass beneath you. An ant industriously makes its way through the jungle of green stalks. Up and down and up and down he goes. How big the outdoors must seem to him! You lie in the grass again. . . . An hour has slipped away.

Suddenly you feel so close to the outdoors and nature herself that you think for a moment you can feel the great heart of the earth beating beneath you. How magical it is, how real it seems, how fleeting the impression. You can't tell anyone what you feel, for the calipers of perception have no handy scales. It's a solo business this tranquility. And probably better really, for communication of *felt* things is a risky business.

But how grand the moment!

Aerial view looking south across Lyell Glacier and Mt. Lyell. Mt. Maclure and its glacier are at the right. Note the curving terminal moraines and the fact that these glaciers are on the shaded, north sides of the peaks.

14

YOSEMITE VALLEY TO DONOHUE PASS
Lyell Glacier

In places where the winter snowfall is greater than the amount of snow that melts during the summer we find areas of permanent snow called *snowfields*. At the lower limit of a snowfield is the *snow line,* above which glacial ice may form in sheltered areas. The position of the snow line varies considerably with the climate. In polar lands the snow line may be even with sea level while near the equator it may lie at elevations of 15,000 to 18,000 feet.

After snow has been on the ground for a time, its light fluffy mass changes into a heavy, granular material called *firn,* which when compacted under pressure becomes glacial ice.

Streams of ice that inch downward through river valleys are called *valley glaciers.* They vary greatly in length, width, and thickness. One branch of the Hubbard Glacier in Alaska is 75 miles long while many of the Sierra Nevada glaciers measure less than a quarter of a mile. A *piedmont glacier* is formed by two or more valley glaciers that flow out on a lowland plain and join to make a single body of advancing ice. *Ice sheets* or *ice caps* are enormous mounds of ice that flow radially outward under their own weight and are usually thick enough to bury both the high and low features of the land on which they lie. The Vatna Glacier in Iceland for example, measures about 75 by 100 miles, is 750 feet thick, and discharges in many directions.[1]

A glacier flows downward from above the snow-line until it moves into an area where it begins to melt and evaporate. When the climate grows colder or more snow falls, the glacier advances. With warmer weather or less snow, the ice mass retreats. During our lifetime the earth has been undergoing a warm climatic cycle and glaciers throughout the world have been wasting away. In the recent past, however, glaciers have advanced significantly. During the Middle Ages the climate was milder than today and farming was carried on in some European areas now covered by ice. In the valley of Chamonix, France, for instance, a silver mine was buried by an advancing glacier, and the village of St. Jean de Perthuis has been covered by the Brenva Glacier since 1600.[2]

Glaciers move a few inches or feet per day which can be demonstrated by placing a row of stakes across the front. All the stakes will move, those toward the center of the ice going the fastest. We can see by the color, composition, or shape of rocks on top of a glacier that they often have been carried a long distance by the moving ice. And we know that a glacier heavily scratches the rock surfaces over which it moves by the striations and polish left when it retreats or melts.

Different sections of a glacier move at varying speeds. There are two main zones of movement: an upper brittle zone 100 to 200 feet thick and a lower zone where the ice assumes a plastic or semi-fluid form because of the pressure from above. The lower zone of flow moves faster than the brittle zone above, causing fractures, cracks, and deep *crevasses.* A glacier moves most rapidly at its center a little above the valley floor, for the sides and bottom of the ice are retarded by friction against the valley floor and walls.

A valley glacier moves great quantities of earth materials. Rocks broken loose from adjacent cliffs by frost action clatter down on the ice. Snowbanks and landslides avalanche onto the surface, bringing piles of rocks and rubble. The moving ice carries all these materials along, transporting them long distances. As we have seen, when a glacier moves across fractured or jointed rock it rips out large blocks by quarrying or plucking, a process helped by the re-freezing of meltwater which runs into cracks and becomes solidly frozen to the bottom of the ice which continuing to move may bodily tear out the block.

The head of a valley glacier rests against a mountain, but in moving, the ice pulls slightly away from the wall of the cliff, making a deep crack called a *bergschrund*. During daylight hours, meltwater runs into the bergschrund. At night it freezes and expands in cracks in the cliff wall. Chunks of the mountain wall are gradually torn out by a combination of plucking and frost action and begin to move away with the glacier. In ages of time this action at the head of the glacier erodes into the mountain itself, making a glacial amphitheater or a cirque.

Cirques are very characteristic of mountainous areas and one of the most notable features of the Sierra Nevada. After a glacier has melted, the cirque is left as a large, vertical-walled bowl with the side away from the mountain cut open. Often the floor of a cirque is lower than its opening lip and a lake or lakes are inside. The knife edges along many peaks were formed by steep-walled glacial cirques which eroded toward one another from different directions and finally joined or partially joined to make jagged, serrated walls.

The enormous heap of rocks and earth rubble deposited at the foot of a glacier is called a *terminal moraine*, a crescent-shaped wall of glacial till that marks the limit of the glacier's advance. The ridge may be 25 to several hundred feet high and is the place where glacial melting and glacial advance exactly balance. As the ice melts, the rocks are left and the terminal moraine grows. If a glacier retreats, a series of smaller recessional moraines are laid down, each marking a place where the glacier was stabilized for a time. Rubble collected along the side of a glacier is a *lateral moraine*. When two glaciers join, their lateral moraines combine into a *medial moraine* which flows out on the surface of the resulting larger ice stream, making a dark streak on the surface of the ice. On complicated glaciers the whole surface of the ice may be covered with rocks and debris.

When a glacier fails to move for some years, a large moraine-like structure may build up which is really a heavy wall of ice layered over with insulating rock debris. Many such ice-cored moraines are found in the Sierra and may last for centuries.[4]

Both the sides and bottom of a glacier are eroding forces and the resulting valley is always U-shaped, rather than V-shaped as from a stream. The U-shaped valley has steep or vertical walls and tributary streams plunge over the edges, forming high leaping waterfalls, as in Yosemite and Tehipite Valleys.

Every glacier has melting ice, and a stream always issues from its foot, carrying down a load of pulverized rock suspended in the water. This glacial flour gives glacial streams and lakes a characteristic milky-green coloration.

Today glaciers cover about ten per cent of the land area of the world. Though they are widely scattered—even being found on Mt. Kenya in East Africa almost astride the equator—some 96 per cent of the ice is concentrated in Greenland and Antarctica. In the past however, great ice sheets covered large sections of the earth and existing glaciers extended far past their present limits. Geologists tell us that within the past 1,000,000 years there have been four significant ice advances, the last covering nearly 27 per cent of the land area of the world. During the period of maximum glaciation the level of the sea was 350 to 400 feet lower than it is now since much of the earth's water was then locked in ice and snow. But periods of glaciation go back much further—to 230 and 600 million years ago—and tell us that the tide of warm and cold cycles has been with us since the dawn of the earth itself.

Glacial polish.

15

YOSEMITE VALLEY TO DONOHUE PASS
Rosy Finch, Bird of the Ice and Snow

The true mountaineer among birds is the rosy finch or leucosticte, a purplish seedeater the size of a sparrow who thrives in a life zone most animals shun. This lively, friendly bird takes his living from patches of alpine turf along the margins of high lakes and streams and from the ice and snow itself where tiny seeds and insects are deposited by winds that swirl up from the lowlands. Often you find him on fields of snow and glaciers that have melted back during warm periods to expose frozen insects and preserved seeds. He seems quite happy to catch small insects on the fly or to gather those that have fallen or melted out of the snow. He's fat, dainty, moves with alacrity, and you see him everywhere.

The male rosy finch has a body of chocolate-brown with scarlet or rosy-edged feathers on the foreparts of his wings, rump, tail and sides. The top of his head is black in front and light grey behind. The colors of the female are similar except that she is more drab with not as much red and a less conspicuous grey patch on her head. Each has a sort of protective snowmask of tiny feathers over its nostrils. Their call is a rather loud coarse chirp. At a glance the rosy finches seem like good-sized sparrows with a reddish wash on their bodies but here the resemblance ends, for the finches are far more active and often dart about the high cliffs and snowfields in large twittering groups, racing together, turning and undulating, almost disappearing, and then rushing back to land for a moment before they are off again. You get the feeling from watching them that they really love to fly and like to show off their prowess.

Usually they have their alpine world all to themselves and scarcely tolerate other birds.

". . . Here came a mad band of some fifty rosy finches chasing a sharp-shinned hawk off their mountain," wrote Charles Harwell. "The hawk made no attempt to do anything but escape. We watched the chase disappear over Parker Pass; then in a few minutes the victors returned. Now their flight was more undulating, they were in smaller groups, they were less noisy. We watched them with a sort of proud interest as they disappeared around an arête and we knew they would soon be busy hopping around over their home icefield, gathering whatever seeds the winds might have scattered there, or whatever frozen insects might conveniently have melted out that day."[1]

The rosy finches hide their nests well, putting them deep in crevices in cliffs or far back under large piled-up rocks on steep talus slopes. As a rule the nests are in deep shade which is cold and damp but the birds don't seem to mind. The finches are gregarious and often four or five fly together on food hunting expeditions which makes it hard to follow an individual or pair to a nest. In fact the nesting habits of the rosy finch were unknown to science until 1910, when a nest was discovered near the summit of Pyramid Peak in the northern Sierra.[2]

The six to seven inch nest is thick-walled and neat, and tightly constructed of dried grasses, mosses, shreds of bark, and tiny roots. Sometimes it is lined with fine grass or feathers and scratched into the thin soil which may be under the rocks. One brood is raised each year from four to five pure white eggs which are laid in June or July. The strong winds that blow around the nests often make the feeding chores of the adults doubly hard, but like parents everywhere they find that perseverance is the answer.[3]

Several years ago an alert observer noticed a pair of rosy finches nesting on a ledge three inches wide 20 feet down in a vertical mine shaft at 11,000 feet near Gaylor Lakes in Yosemite.[4] Vernon Bailey, chief field naturalist of the old U. S. Biological Survey investigated a nesting site at Rodgers Lake:

YOSEMITE VALLEY TO DONOHUE PASS

"The nest was about six feet from the base of a narrow chimney or cleft that dropped from the north face of the peak," wrote Bailey. "Here, at 10,000 feet, on a cold slope, there were snowbanks on both sides. By piling up a few rocks we could look right into the nest and see the three young birds. . . . The nest was made of coarse sticks and roots and turf, well matted in thick walls and lined with soft grass fibers and placed on a little shelf back in the half darkness of the crack. It was well planned to withstand cold weather and rough storms, but not so sheltered as most of the nests are. On the cliff above we saw dozens of the birds carrying nesting material or food into cracks and caverns that were mostly inaccessible, and always out of sight. These were all above the snowbanks at the base of the cliff, but the birds often came down to the snowbanks to feed or drink, and were carrying food and nest material from the heather beds below. . . . The mother bird did most of the feeding and at times brooded the young, but the male also brought food and did his best to try to draw us away from the nest."[5]

Our little friend seems a fearless bird and regards people with curiosity. He does not hesitate to come close. "A pair perched on a log within eight feet of us, eyed us intently, and hopped all over our bedding and clothes inspecting us thoroughly," wrote Joseph Dixon.[6]

The rosy finch evidently stays in his high mountain habitat all year-round, except during the most severe storms when he descends a few thousand feet. On the east side of the Sierra the birds have been seen briefly at the foot of the mountains, but on the western slopes they seldom come down to even 8,000 feet.[7] Their arctic life zone lies above the region of maximum snowfall, and the winds and moderate temperatures[8] free much of the high landscape from snow so the finches may live quite comfortably. To my knowledge no one has ever gone to the high peaks in winter expressly looking for this hardy little fellow. What evidence we have, however, indicates that he stays in his arctic world all winter, fearlessly and strongly flying in his mountaintop world and truly earning the title *the bird of the ice and snow.*

At left, Rosy finch, Lyell Glacier, and Mt. Lyell. The long horizontal crack between the glacier and the mountain is a bergschrund.

16

DONOHUE PASS TO SILVER PASS
How it all Began

About 200 million years ago the land now covered by the Sierra Nevada was the bed of a shallow bay of the Pacific Ocean that then flooded and ebbed over much of present-day California. Enormous quantities of mud, silt and sand had been washing into this area from nearby higher land for a very long time and had compacted into layers thousands of feet deep, far below the surface of the sea. Debris from skeletons of billions of tiny marine animals formed beds of lime which lay among the other sediments.

At this time—which geologists call the Permian Epoch—all these sediments below the Pacific were uplifted and folded into mountains from tremendous pressures deep within the earth. The mud, silt, sand, and lime became slate, shale, sandstone, and limestone which formed the new range that cast its morning shadow on the ocean to the west.

During the next 50 to 100 million years this first range was slowly eroded away to hills and ridges. Most of its rocky material gradually washed into the sea where it again accumulated in tremendous layers. This time beds of volcanic material—layers of cinders and pumice—were mixed in with the slate, shale and other minerals. Finally the region sank beneath the sea completely.

About 130 million years ago these layers under the sea were again folded and uplifted after being invaded with molten granite from far within the earth and for a second time were folded and wrinkled and pushed up into rows of parallel mountains that trended to the northwest. During the next 50 million years several thousand feet of soft, sedimentary material was washed into the sea and the mountains became hills. Granite was uncovered over large areas.

Some 60 million years ago these hills began to be uplifted together with the country to the east. The streams now ran faster and cut deeply into the hills which began to look like low mountains. Volcanoes erupted in the northern part and repeatedly spread lava and ash. Volcanic mud poured from fissures and craters near the crest and flowed westward, burying some valleys in the north. Then 12 to 15 million years ago the Sierra was uplifted several thousand feet more. This movement tilted the whole enormous block range toward the west and southwest. For the next five million years all was quiet, except for the streams running to the west which cut deep, broad valleys. Then about eight million years ago there was further tilting to the west and more uplifting which pushed the crest of the range to over 14,000 feet. Along with the tilting, strong faulting or shearing movements caused the east side to drop, giving the Sierra Nevada its characteristic form: gentle slopes on the west; precipitous drops to the east.

The great Ice Age began one million years ago, the first of four successive eras of ice and snow and perpetual winter. The range was almost entirely covered with glaciers which carved and brought into shape the mountains that we know today. The valleys on the western slope were deepened into canyons, both by the rivers and by the glaciers. After the first Ice Age there were more faulting movements on the eastern edge of the range, causing the Great Basin to sink further which gave even more emphasis to the great block of the Sierra Nevada. About 9,000 years ago the glaciers of the last Ice Age melted when temperatures rose. The small glaciers that exist in the Sierra today were formed during the last 3,000 years.[1]

You might reasonably ask how geologists date these vast epochs and disturbances that extend so far back in time. Dating is done in two ways. Biologic evidence consists of analyzing the remains of animals and plants found in sedimentary rocks.

Aerial view northeast across the black eminence of Banner Peak (12,945). Thousand Island Lake at left; Garnet Lake at right. Mono Lake and the Mono Craters are at the upper left.

Most fossil remains are of plants or animals now extinct and as scientists go back in time, the remains go from fossils clearly related to living species to increasingly primitive forms. From mammals the record goes back to dinosaurs, to small reptiles, salamander-like amphibians, fish, and finally fossils of invertebrate animals like the trilobite, an extinct marine creature whose remains look something like a horseshoe crab. Paleontologists have been able to construct a time scale and by examining fossils can reasonably tell the age of the rock in which they occur.

Radioactive dating is newer and in many ways extremely exciting. It is used to find the ages of rocks millions of years old. The technique is based on the fact that radioactive elements slowly disintegrate into lead. From the time a mineral with a trace of uranium is formed from molten rock, the uranium commences to break up into lead. The rate of disintegration of uranium is known and it is possible to calculate the age of a rock by computing the amount of lead relative to the amount of uranium still present. This can be done with great accuracy. An isotope of carbon is used to date rocks up to 35,000 years old. With the exception of a certain marine shale in Sweden, radioactive dating can only be done with igneous rocks since sedimentary materials have no radioactive particles.[2]

If we examine geological evidence we can answer the puzzling question of why so many streams in the Sierra run parallel with the range, that is northwest or southeast when by reason and common sense all streams should flow down the mountains. Why does the Middle Fork of the San Joaquin flow south for 14 miles before it turns westward? Why does the South Fork of the San Joaquin flow northwest for over 40 miles behind Kaiser Ridge before turning toward the west? What is the reason the Lyell Fork of the Tuolumne goes northwest? Why does the Merced River flow northwestward near Mt. Clark?

The answer is that 130 million years ago the ancestral Sierra Nevada was worn down to low hills and ridges which trended northwest. These hills and ridges were of more resistant rock and the rivers ran even with them in parallel valleys where the rock was softer and weaker. When the Sierra block began to be uplifted, these streams cut deeper and deeper into the sedimentary strata and finally even into the underlying granite.

As the range continued to rise and the western slope grew steeper, new streams began to run down its face. In time these rivers cut back into the range and coalesced with the already formidable canyons of the northwest and southeast running streams. Today we see that a good many Sierra streams still run in these ancient streambeds and we can readily view the areas where the streams change direction to flow in the newer—geologically speaking—streambeds.

DONOHUE PASS TO SILVER PASS
Meadow Building

This is a photograph of shoreline meadow on the edge of Thousand Island Lake near its inlet. The water over the rocks is several inches deep but so clear that you can hardly see it. The month is July; as the surrounding snows melt off and the lake drains a bit the water will get very shallow here and perhaps dry up entirely. But now the water is running surprisingly fast along the edge of the very thick, soft, wet, and spongy grass which hangs over the shoreline rocks in undulating mounds and billows that curve down to the water. In some places the heavy sod has grown across rocks while the water continues to run underneath a dozen feet or more from shore. As you eat your lunch you can hear the water under the meadow tinkling and gurgling, a lovely sound, but mysterious in a way for you're not quite sure from where it's coming. Sometimes you can put your hand on the grass over the running water and feel its vibrations beneath the rich loam.

The rocks here are fragments of glacier deposited granite that have been fractured by frost action and have settled into mosaic-like patterns. Sediment has collected in the cracks between the rocks but their surfaces are swept free of particles by the current. When the water level drops in the late summer, seeds fall on the sandy grit along the edges and cracks and lie in the mud for a time, sprouting if they're not drowned or dried out.

Tiny triangular-stalked sedges begin to grow if the water level is just right, and in time build turf, thick mats of intertwined roots and stems. The last sentence took only a minute to write but one inch of the turf we are discussing may take 50 years or more to form. The growth starts from accumulations of sediments which favor sproutings, and the sedges and sometimes rushes advance outward, climbing over low rocks and bridging to other outgrowing centers. As the turf increases in thickness it becomes drier at the top and attracts grasses and flowers that require less moisture. At the bottom of the photograph are four tiny white five-petalled flowers of cinquefoil, indicative of drier conditions.

All this growth restricts the water and makes the current run faster in the narrow channels. The current sweeps against some of the turf, especially on the concave sides of curves where the water runs faster, and undercuts the plant material which here measures between five and six inches thick. Freezing and thawing on the edges of the turf may also restrict growth and keep the borders smooth. Even in August the noon temperature of the water measured only 41°F. and on many nights a wrinkle of ice forms along the edges.

If the meadow is very wet and bog-like, conditions may be favorable for the growth of sphagnum. If the weather is not too cold and there is sufficient moisture, algae may grow, but here the sun dries out the grass on top and the 9,834-foot altitude is too cold to encourage much algae. Someday the grasses may expand and cover more of the lake and make a large meadow. But this process is extremely slow and quite unsuccessful in many places. It is true that many Sierra meadows were once lakes but all Sierra lakes will not become meadows (unless man keeps tampering with natural processes). I often hear people discussing how this lake "will shortly be filled in." I suppose this is because it is easy to see old lake boundaries in many existing meadows. But plenty of lakes, especially active ones with heavy flows and fluctuating water levels, are thousands of years old and show little indication of change. The seeds of change are present — the bits of meadow around the lakes — but once a stable, climax condition is reached, the border between the lake and meadow fragments stays very much the same.

Devils Postpile (above). Jumbled pile of toppled columns. At right is a close-up of vertical columns showing the peculiar forms that basalt takes when it cools from a molten state.

DONOHUE PASS TO SILVER PASS
Devils Postpile

About eight million years ago the mass of the Sierra Nevada was sharply accented when its eastern side began to drop and sheer away, leaving a steep and precipitous eastern wall. These strong faulting actions created openings and passageways deep within the earth, and hot volcanic materials erupted over a long time. From Mono Lake to Fish Valley, south of the Red Cones, a distance of 27 miles in a perfect north-south line, igneous material burst to the surface as gas, dust, ash, cinders, bombs, blocks, and lava.

Two to five million years ago the volcanic action built Mammoth Mountain whose remnant summit is now 11,053 feet high.[1] Later, frothy pumice fragments exploded from a series of 30 cones just east of the Sierra proper; most of the pumice came down around the volcanic pipes but some was carried by winds and deposited in places to depths of 2,000 feet. Hot springs flowed at Reds Meadow and Fish Valley. Superheated gases and sulphurous fumes issued from vents; soda springs began to bubble. Obsidian flowed on the surface at Glass Creek and south of Mono Lake. Pumice dust rained down along the Middle Fork of the San Joaquin and formed extensive pumice flats, burying trees and cliffs and re-routing creeks.[2]

Between 100,000 and 200,000 years ago, basaltic lava poured into the valley of the Middle Fork of the San Joaquin River for at least six miles and piled up to depths of 100 to 700 feet. As the lava cooled it shrank. The vertical shrinkage was taken care of by gravity but the horizontal contractions produced tensions that forced the basalt to crack. The gray molten rock was almost pure and as it cooled, the stresses tended to make three cracks at 120° to each other, radiating out from centers 12 to 30 inches apart. The cracks grew until they joined each other, making four, five, six and seven-sided figures where the cracks touched. As the

Where glaciers rode over the vertical basalt columns, the ice polished their ends and fully revealed their polygonal forms.

lava cooled and shrank downward, the polygonal patterns followed deep into the main body of the rock, creating odd-looking columns as big around as a man and as high as 60 feet. Where the cooling was irregular, the stresses bent and twisted the columns.

The basalt came after the third glacial flow but prior to the fourth and last ice advance, the Wisconsin Stage. This 1,000-foot-thick glacier inched its way down the river valley and ripped into the columnar basalt which was easily quarried away since the columns were already cracked and standing like wheat stalks waiting for a threshing machine. Only in one place was the basalt resistant enough to withstand the ice. That remnant is preserved today as Devils Postpile National Monument, proclaimed by President Taft in 1911, a small enclave along the river, 2½ miles long and 880 yards wide. At the southern end of the monument the Middle Fork of the San Joaquin tumbles over a basalt cliff to form Rainbow Fall, a smooth avalanche of water 140 feet high.

Where the ice rode over the basalt columns and clipped off the tops of the posts, it polished and shined the flat surfaces into a patterned, mosaic floor. Here you can see the scratches and polish, some of which has worn away from the soft rock during the 20,000 years the glacier has been gone. It's the best place to inspect the cracks in the basalt and see how they radiated from centers to make the polygonal columns.

Number of sides of basalt polygons	per cent occurrence (based on 200 samples)
4	2
5	37
6	55½
7	5½

Frost action between the columns has toppled perhaps a thousand of the stone fingers into a huge talus pile along the east side of the river. The top parts of some of the columns lean as much as 12 inches from others and seem ready to fall at the touch of a finger. However, comparison today with photographs taken in 1909 show the columns standing exactly the same. In 1952, the region was shaken by a moderately strong earthquake which might have been expected to have brought down a dozen or more of the leaning columns. The ranger staff looked long and hard but reported no new toppled columns, once again indicating the slowness of geological change.

Differential stresses during and after column formation caused these strangely opposing curves.

(*opposite page*) Top — Marmot just prior to hibernation in the fall. Center — Hummingbird photographed near Florence Lake. Bottom — Frog, Rae Lakes.

Rainbow Falls, two views

Red Cones

Though scientists tell us the cones are dormant and have been for thousands of years you somehow expect rumbling, smoke, and fire when you approach these great piles of reddish cinders. Even animals regard the cones with caution, sniffing and pawing, and seem uneasy and glad to get away to the real forest and mountains again. Each of the two cones is symmetrical with a small crater at the top where the porous volcanic materials once spewed forth. Now the cones are quiet and graced only by a few poorly-rooted pines that bravely try to march up the dry slopes.

19

DONOHUE PASS TO SILVER PASS
Golden Trout

When cattlemen and sheepherders took their hungry animals to the alpine meadows of the Kern River in the early 1870s they found a strange trout in the streams near their camps. Like other trout it was wary, full of life, quick and energetic, and eternally hungry for choice insects. But here the resemblance stopped, for the trout was colored like no other fish the herders had ever seen.

The top of the head and the back of the trout were a shiny olive-green. Its belly glistened with a midline strip of crimson, while its dorsal and caudal fins were olive, heavily peppered with large black dots. The lower fins were reddish, the rear ones edged with white. Most surprising of all, the sides of the trout glowed with flashing slashes of crimson-gold overlaid with a row of 10 or 12 faint oval-shaped greyish patches. The fish was gorgeous!

A few vague reports came out of the mountains about the beauty and gameness of the fish but the actual existence of the trout seemed more based on rumor than reality until 1875 when Professor H. W. Henshaw saw the species in the South Fork of the Kern River and noted: " . . . in the clear, rapid current of the mountain stream a flash of sunlight is scarcely quicker than the gleam of gold and silver seen for a single instant as the whirling waters are cut by one of these trout as he makes a rush from his lurking place for some chance morsel that is being borne past him."[1]

In 1893, Dr. David Starr Jordan, the president of Stanford University, received three specimens of the new trout that were caught in Cottonwood Creek on the east side of the Sierra about eight miles south of Mt. Whitney. Dr. Jordan described the fish and named it *Salmo mykiss agua-bonita*.

Ten years later the writer Stewart Edward White visited the Kern Plateau and was so impressed with the beauty of the fish and the ease with which it could be exterminated that he asked President Theodore Roosevelt to intervene. The President directed the Commissioner of Fisheries to investigate and during the summer of 1904 three scientists and an artist under the direction of Dr. Barton W. Evermann explored various branches of the Kern River, including Volcano Creek, later to be named Golden Trout Creek.

The following winter Evermann published a lengthy report describing the country and the fish his party had found. He verified the *Salmo agua-bonita* that Jordan had named 12 years before and in addition claimed two new species, *Salmo whitei* from Soda Creek, and *Salmo roosevelti* from Volcano Creek. Since Cottonwood Creek had originally been barren of fish, Evermann made inquiries to find out how these waters draining to the east had been planted.

"The golden trout were caught in South Fork of Kern River in a little stream in Mulky Meadow just where the Hockett trail enters the Meadow," wrote Judge A. C. Harvey of Lone Pine. "They were caught with hook and line by S. V. Stevens, A. D. Stevens, and Thomas George. Thirteen fish were caught and carried in a coffee pot over the Hockett trail and put in Cottonwood Creek about a mile above the Stevens sawmill. . . . This was, I think, in July, 1876."[2]

Evermann suggested that rigid restrictions on fishing be adopted, including a minimum size, a limit to the number that one person might catch, and a prohibition of fishing during the spawning season. He reported the golden trout to be unusually hardy and suggested planting them in small, clear mountain streams throughout the West.

Since the days of Dr. Evermann, scientists have come to realize that many varieties of fish thought to have been separate species are really the same

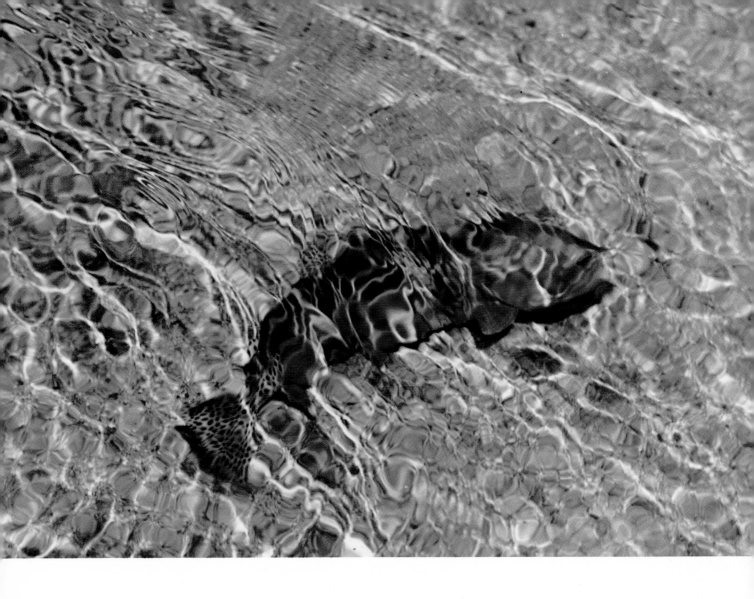

basic fish. Today the golden trout is considered to be one species, *Salmo aguabonita.* Taxonomists however do recognize two sub-species, the South Fork of Kern golden trout *(Salmo aguabonita aguabonita),* and the Little Kern golden trout *(Salmo aguabonita whitei).*[3] It is quite difficult for the ordinary person to distinguish these sub-species. Even Dr. Evermann was exasperated. "An examination of the large series of specimens shows them to be a very perplexing lot," he wrote when discussing the *whitei* from Coyote Creek. "The amount of variation among them is very great, and it is not without hesitation that I refer them all provisionally to *Salmo whitei.*"[4]

The closeness of the varieties of golden may be because two of Evermann's three species were taken from streams that were joined together at one time.[5] Perhaps time will erase even the sub-species of today, for the golden trout has been widely planted throughout the Sierra and readily interbreeds with rainbow trout. A thousand variations of color now flourish in the high waters of the range.[6]

The golden trout is generally a small fish, six to ten inches in length, although specimens as large as 18 inches have been taken from Sierra lakes. The fish does best in waters above 9,000 feet where the summer water temperatures seldom exceed 55° though in a few places the temperature climbs as high as 65°.[7] (The temperature of the water was 42° when the accompanying photographs were made.) The principal foods of the trout are immature caddis and midge flies and tiny water fleas.

Every year in June and July, Fish and Game workers from the State of California take about 500,000 eggs (500 to 600 per female) from golden trout specially trapped at various lakes on Cottonwood Creek. The eggs, more delicate than those of any other trout, are reared at the Mt. Whitney and Hot Creek hatcheries and the fingerlings distributed widely. The eggs take about 20 days to hatch when kept at 58° and another 18 days or so for the yolk-sac to be absorbed. In the wild, the trout spawn at much lower temperatures (often just as the ice goes off the lakes) and the incubation time of the eggs is considerably longer. At 40° for example, it takes over 40 days for the eggs to hatch. Growth is rapid the first summer and native fry double their weight every two weeks.[8]

The flesh of the golden is usually white when taken from streams, and pinkish when caught in lakes because the lake diet includes tiny red copepods, scuds, and other freshwater crustaceans which also color the eggs a deep salmon pink.[9] The age of the fish depends on many things but one study showed five years to be the normal life span for a lake golden.[10]

Camping . . .

. . . and more
camping

20

DONOHUE PASS TO SILVER PASS
Glenn Burns, Packer

Glenn Burns has packed people and supplies into the wilds of the Sierra Nevada for 45 summers and he'd rather lead a string of mules up a switch-back trail and over the divide to the next camp than eat. "That is unless it's eating deep-fried trout around a campfire," he says with a mischievous grin. "This high country life sort of gets in your blood and once it does you're not good for much."

Glenn was born in California's San Joaquin Valley in the foothills near Clovis. He began ranching when he was 16, running 15 Arizona heifers on rented land. As he learned the cattle business he increased his herd and bought property with the proceeds of his ranching and summertime packing until today he owns 2300 acres and keeps 150 to 300 cattle, depending on the market and range conditions. These days he mixes up his herd with Shorthorns, Herefords, Brahmas, and Santa Gertrudis stock. Glenn operates his spread by himself, herding his cattle from horseback with the help of a well-trained border collie. Like all ranchers he spends a lot of time mending fences and tries to check all his posts and barbed wire twice a year. In addition to his own land he rents another 2,000 acres of natural pasture and 40 acres of irrigated grass. He has a son and daughter and three grand-children. His wife seldom goes to the mountains; she stays home to watch the ranch and cattle.

The same year he began ranching—1920—Glenn hired out to lead strings of mules into the High Sierra during the summer. The fishermen and hunt-ers and hikers Glenn has packed in include Boy Scouts, young ladies for girls' camps, college pro-fessors, retired lawyers, doctors, plumbers, police-men—the rich and the poor, the young and the old, the weak and the sturdy. His mules have hauled provisions for trail crews, cement and steel cable for bridges, the bodies of crashed fliers, power saws and roofing for snow survey cabins, drilling equip-ment for dam engineers, fish for planting in remote lakes, and tens of thousands of duffel bags.

"The people I've seen come to the Sierra Ne-vada over the years are much the same," says Glenn. "They travel here because they like the land and enjoy the high mountain out-of-doors. Of course things have become more fancy. In the old days we used bed rolls instead of sleeping bags and we never thought of bringing in a stove.

"The country has changed more than the peo-ple and I'm sure sorry to see it," he says. "The wilderness is getting smaller all the time. In the old days it might take two or three days to pack into a place. Now there's hardly a camp that's less than a day-and-a-half from a road end. Jeep tracks are sneaking up each side of the Sierra.

"And the regulations and rules are getting more strict all the time," says Glenn. "It used to be that you didn't see a park ranger or forester all summer. Now they're in all the big meadows, hanging up signs, nosing around, and making a big fuss. A fellow doesn't mind following orders from a man who knows the grazing game, but taking orders from 20-year-old wonders who have studied only from textbooks or from someone back in an office who doesn't even come out to look is hard to take for an old goat like me."

Glenn is a medium-sized, lean, leathery man slightly cricked from long years in the saddle. He wears Levi pants and a dark blue western shirt, but he doesn't wear his Levi jacket unless it's downright cold. "If I wore the jacket in the summer what would I put on during deer season?" His deeply-tanned face is shaded by an $18 wide-brimmed Don Hoy hat and he wears boots and spurs when riding; otherwise heavy work shoes.

Glenn is a shy and retiring cowboy with a soft, low-pitched voice. He speaks slowly and sincerely

GLENN BURNS, PACKER

with uncommon courtesy and is never too busy to chat. His reticent manner—typically Scottish—belies his considerable knowledge of lakes, trails, passes, and animal wranglers in the Sierra. He has a wonderful sense of the right joke at the apt moment. (Comment at evening chow to a group of vacationing nurses: "I went down to the blood bank to give a pint of blood and the nurse said 'Go hop in bed and I'll be right with you.' Gosh, I didn't know what to do.")

Glenn knows dozens of cowboy songs and with prodding will sing, delivering his cowboy ballads in a thin, waspish voice in a kind of chant, relying on dozens of humorous verses for the effect he always gets.

He ran his own summer and fall pack station from 1926 to 1954 when he sold it. At the end he had enough business to use 140 head of stock. His best year was 1944, when he cleared $11,000 after expenses. He is proud that all his business came from word of mouth from satisfied customers since he never advertised. "I got sick and tired of forest service regulations so I sold out," he says. "Also it got hard to get help. Now I just take trips that interest me."

Today Glenn has about 30 head of pack stock, mostly mules, and still has the reputation of having the best stock in the mountains. He treats his animals gently, feeds them a little barley each morning to keep them happy, sees that they're well shod, and doesn't overload them. Except for the summer packing and riding, his stock runs on his ranch "free and loose like birds." Glenn has had some of his mules 20 years and all the horses and mules know one another and like to stay together.

When he packs now he generally has two or more assistants, depending on the size of the party. He gets up at 5 or 5:30 and goes out tracking his stock which may be nearby (the bells on the mares softly clanking) or can have wandered four or five miles, depending on the grazing and temperature. Even with hobbles on the mares a cold night keeps the animals moving. After the stock is in, the packers have breakfast and start breaking up camp, stowing all the gear into large wooden kyacks, one of which is hung from each side of a mule's saddle. Then mounted on horseback and each leading four or five mules the packers are off to the next camp. They carry no lunch and ride non-stop, perhaps ten miles and five or six hours away. Once there the stock is quickly unloaded and a bucket of Kool-Aid is made to wash down lunch.

"Ahhhh Kool-Aid," says Glenn. "There's nothing finer after a long trail than a dipperful of Kool-Aid. Here—have some more."

21

DONOHUE PASS TO SILVER PASS
Snow, Silver Pass

The greatest blessing of the Sierra Nevada is its long winter when the land is largely protected from man and can recover to begin fresh and new. The enormity of snow that falls on the Sierra is not generally known, even to most Californians. Near Lake Tahoe, at 6,000 to 7,000 feet, the annual snowfall totals 30 to 40 feet. In some winters it reaches 60 feet and as much as 32 feet has fallen in a single month. During the winter of 1906-7, the weatherman in the little town of Tamarack, at 8,000 feet in Alpine County, just south of Lake Tahoe, amazed the world with an official report of 73 feet, enough—if it fell at one time—to cover a five-story building. This record stood until 1953-54 when 80 feet of snowfall was measured at Thompson Pass in Alaska.

The average fall for the snowiest parts of the Sierra is 37 feet; by March 15 there is still 12 to 17 feet remaining. The heaviest snowfall ever recorded anywhere was on January 19, 1933, when the astonished rangers at Sequoia National Park watched five feet of new snow descend on Giant Forest in one night.[1]

During the winter of 1928-29, a hardy soul named Orland Bartholomew skied along the entire route of the John Muir Trail. He left Lone Pine on December 25 and arrived in Yosemite Valley on April 3. Bartholomew carried a 60-pound pack that he replenished from food and equipment caches that he had stored in 11 places along the trail the previous autumn.

Such a trip might seem hazardous to the point of foolhardiness but Bartholomew reported no discomfort or trouble. Obviously a superb skier and well experienced in the craft of camping on snow, Bartholomew was surprised by the relatively mild winter at the high altitude of the John Muir Trail. He had expected the temperature to decrease with the altitude but it didn't; he noted instead no temperature below 0°F. above 11,000 feet during the entire winter. The average snowpack did not exceed four feet and southern exposures of rock and canyons were often entirely bare of snow and ice. This was due, he suggested, to the high temperatures and the relatively warm winds. He took high and low temperatures at 17 locations which averaged 35.3 maximum and 9.4 minimum, but when he descended to an area protected from the winds at 10,300 feet on Tyndall Creek he recorded temperatures as low as -14°.

Bartholomew climbed Whitney on January 10 and found it "crowned only with sand and sunshine." He saw little snow on Mt. Langley above 13,000 feet. He noted that many streams flowed almost unobstructed by ice, even above 10,500 feet. On January 13 he dipped water from a lake on Crabtree Creek at 11,700 feet, and noted on March 4th that the outlet of Evolution Lake was entirely open. Most of the lakes were covered with snow but Lake Marjorie and Wanda Lake were windswept and solidly frozen and overlaid with severely buckled ice.[2]

ɤ　　ɤ　　ɤ

The snow that falls on the Sierra Nevada comes from the Pacific where westerly winds bring winter storms from far out in the ocean. The winds push the storms eastward over the California coast where they stream unimpeded to the mountains. When the warm moisture-laden clouds come in contact with the mass of the Sierra they are forced upward, and cool to lose their moisture as rain and snow. Most of the snow is dumped in the middle regions between 4,000 and 9,000 feet; some comes down all the way to the Sierra crest of course, but less than might be expected. The temperature is colder toward the summits though and snow that does fall lasts much longer, sometimes until the following winter.

During the summer however, practically no rain falls on the Sierra. Storms heading for California from the west are blocked by a high pressure area far out in the Pacific that moves northward in the summer and deflects storms to Oregon and Washington. In addition the high pressure area sends out stronger winds which strike California from the northwest, forcing the south-flowing ocean current along the coast to move faster which causes it to upwell, bringing colder water to the surface. When the moist ocean air strikes the cold water, immense fogs result. Finally the summer sun heats the San Joaquin Valley to the west of the Sierra to high temperatures—often exceeding 100°—which provide an effective barrier to any moisture-laden air from the Pacific. (The only moisture that gets to the Sierra in the summer is from a rare mass of moist air that sometimes comes from the Gulf of Mexico.) The result of all this is very dry weather in the Sierra except for occasional thundershowers; rainless periods of three or four months are common.[3]

The astounding climatic contrast between summer and winter is perhaps the main reason for the beauty of the Sierra Nevada. The winter brings snow and moisture; the summer brings sun and warmth. Together they nurture superb trees and flowers and meadows in an atmosphere of bounteous lakes and streams and running water, a place where every day is bright and sun-filled and you can sleep without a tent for months. Few places in the world have such contrasts of climate.

The snow that falls on the Sierra Nevada makes it the source of the greatest river system within the boundaries of any single state in the United States. In fact without the range and its snow, California would be a community of villages along the sea with a great inland desert separating it from the rest of America.

"The economic value of Sierra snows is practicably incalculable," writes Professor Richard Joel Russell. "About 60 per cent of the farms in California are irrigated, half of them by water from surface channels. Crop yields vary mainly according to mountain snowfall accumulation and melting rates. On various dates, watchful snow-surveyors, like auditors, issue reports on the balance in reserve. The Sierra holds not only the fortunes of its own inhabitants and of those of valleys on all sides in abeyance for several months of the year, but also those of persons living far away, even in the vicinity of Los Angeles. Practically all of the large metropolitan centers of California depend on Sierra snows for domestic water supply. The lofty oasis of the Far West promotes forest growth, turns climatic desert into productive lands, and brings an abundant life to a large region that otherwise would be unable to support more than a small population."[4]

22

SILVER PASS TO MUIR PASS
Crossing Streams

Perhaps with the exception of solo peak climbing the greatest hazard in the Sierra Nevada is crossing streams. Again and again in the written records of the mountains are accounts of people being drowned. Not novices, newcomers, or first-timers to the mountains always, but experienced rangers, members of trail crews, and packers. Whether from overconfidence, a lack of understanding of the force of swift water, or simple accidents I don't know, but every year there are several obituaries in the local newspapers which conclude: "drowned while crossing a stream."

"We were on horseback riding toward Colby Pass," said Martin Litton, "and had crossed the stream below Colby Lake. It was June and there was still plenty of snow around and of course lots of new ice and frost in the mornings. We crossed the stream some distance above a waterfall on the way up with no difficulty but when we returned in the afternoon the water was a good deal higher and really romping because of melting by the sun.

"The first three men rode across OK and I anticipated no trouble since the water was below the horse's belly and an animal's slender legs present little resistance to the water. But when I was in mid-stream the mule behind me jostled my horse who got excited and stepped off the piled-up rocks of the crossing place. As soon as the deeper water hit the side of the horse it was hopeless and we went over.

"The horse started rolling and I got clear of him but the water was bone-chilling and very swift. I was helpless in the current and was pitched over and over. I don't know how far downstream I went . . . It was all I could do to breathe. I thought my head would be smashed against a rock but the swift water carried me around the rocks to some extent . . . Suddenly I could feel the bottom fall out under me and I thought oh my God! this is the big waterfall! The first thing in my mind was that my backpack was preventing my swimming. It was large and bulky and I had to get out of it. Somehow I pulled one arm out and the pack flipped over my head.

"I saw the banks narrowing and my pack go over the edge of the waterfall," said Litton. "I grabbed for anything. I clawed at clumps of grass, little bushes, driftwood, rocks sticking up—everything I could. Finally when I was about 50 feet from the waterfall there was a big crack in a rock and I jammed my knee into it. The other three men dropped me a rope. I reached for it with my right hand or thought I did but my right arm wasn't there. I felt up my arm and when I got to my shoulder could only feel gristle instead of bone. I got hold of the rope with my other hand and they pulled me up."

Litton almost went out of his mind from pain during the two days it took to get from the remote location to the hospital in Fresno. Doctors put his arm back in its socket but it was more than a year before he regained normal use.

"Though the accident was the horse's fault to some extent because he panicked when pushed by the mule, the fault was mine really for attempting a crossing at all," said Litton, thankful to be alive. "I learned my lesson the hard way. Never again will I underestimate the power of water."

✓ ✓ ✓

The force of moving water is astonishing. When a person wades across a stream his feet, legs, thighs, and possibly his hips are in the water. A little measuring leads to the modest assumption that about two square feet of body surface may be in contact with the water. Hydraulic engineers tell me that there is a loss of drag due to rounded legs and space between the knees and that about 0.6 of two square feet is a better figure. If we calcu-

late the amount of force at various water speeds using the formula* for the dynamic action of flowing water — a mass of water passing a given cross-section in a stream — we come up with the following:

stream speed in miles per hour	force of water in pounds on 1.2 square feet of body surface
1	4.3
3	33
5	103
7	179
10	366
15	926

Because of turbulence from roughness at the bottom of a stream the maximum force of the water is about two-thirds of the distance up from the bottom which means the water tends constantly to upset someone crossing. This force increases rapidly with depth and speed of the water. Of course a man leans upstream into the downstream force by using his muscular power but this in turn is counterbalanced to some extent by the buoyant effect of the water which tends to displace some of his body weight. And if he is leaning upstream and is thrown off balance on a slippery rock he is liable to exert his muscular force momentarily in the opposite direction—downstream—which together with the force of the rushing water will put him in the water.

Once in the stream the force against your body is perhaps quadrupled at once and your weight

advantage is largely lost to the buoyant effect of the water. A crosser needs ample reserve force against the current.

From a glance at the table we see that it is highly advisable to walk some distance out of your way to cross on a bridge (there are 12 on the John Muir Trail) or to hunt for a crossing log when you see white water. It's a good plan to cross above the junction of tributary streams (two easy crossings rather than one hazardous one) and to look for wide shallow places. It's best to cross early in the day and to bridge a stream with rope to hold to. Another help is to use a pole as a downstream crutch or to cross holding hands with someone.

Some people cross barefoot year after year while others—perhaps with more tender feet—carry an old pair of tennis shoes. Another plan is to take off your boots and socks, put your boots back on without socks (which you carry), and wade in your boots. Once across you drain your boots and then put on the dry socks.

$$*F = \frac{QW}{G} \ (V - V_o)$$

F = Force in pounds per sq. ft.
Q = cubic feet per second
W = weight of 1 cubic foot water (62 pounds)
G = gravity (32.16)
V = velocity of water in feet per second
V_o = velocity of moving body in medium.
(assumed to be negligible)

CROSSING STREAMS

Seven Gables

"At a distance of perhaps ten miles from where we first struck the creek the valley ended and the stream forked, its larger branch coming through our pass—a term which we hasten to corrupt to 'impass,'—the smaller draining a remarkable group of chains of lakelets which lay upon a number of terraces, or plateaus, to the south and west. The south wall of the gap we found to be the side of a peak, the eccentric shape of which is suggested in the name Seven Gables, which we hastened to fasten upon it . . . We climbed the Seven Gables on the afternoon of our arrival at the head of the valley—September 20. There was a dash of snow on its chimney-like pinnacle, which must be upwards of 13,600 feet above the sea."

Theodore S. Solomons, writing of his 1894 trip with Leigh Bierce[1]

Lodgepoles and Aspens
South Fork of the San Joaquin

Backpackers . . .

. . . along the trail

Evolution
Valley

123

23

SILVER PASS TO MUIR PASS
Squirrel of the Summits

The most interesting small animal of the Sierra Nevada is the Belding ground squirrel. This dapper chunk of hardy, high-powered spunkiness frisks about the alpine meadows in great colonies, foraging for food among the open patches of bunch grass, sunning himself on the alluvial flats, and playing hide-and-go-seek with his brothers and sisters among the small glacial boulders.

In size he's about like a hamster or guinea pig, a brownish, six-inch furry gentleman with tiny ears, almond-shaped eyes, a rather pointed face, black chin whiskers, and a nose that seems constantly to twitch. He's much given to standing like a soldier at attention when someone strange is around and if that someone makes a move interpreted as suspicious, the Belding is liable to dive into his burrow, though pausing on all fours for a quick look around before plummeting from sight. But like all animals he's curious and if you sit quietly and watch his burrow you'll soon see a pair of beady eyes regarding you, then a head, then the whole, somewhat frightened little fellow, ready to dart back, but cautiously coming out to see who is visiting his domain.

He likes to stand erect on his hind feet, propping himself with his somewhat thin two-inch tail, and peer about his meadow home. It's then that you hear him talk—or rather whistle—a short shrill call accompanied by a slight raising of his head. Other Beldings answer him and soon you see these little brown parcels of inquisitiveness all about you, scampering, frolicking, a circus of tiny animals who forget you are among them until one of them bumps into your shoe and realizes with a start that you are something big and maybe dangerous. Then with a shrill piping of five to eight warning calls the colony stampedes to its burrows, falling all over each other in their haste to hide. The meadow is quiet for a moment, then the little furry heads begin popping above the burrows, and once again the colony is alive, sprinting from hole to hole, whistling raucously, pushing one another, and tumbling and rolling like wild, crazy bumblebees.

The most unusual thing about the Belding is his unique ability to live at such high altitudes, enduring the long and extremely cold winters, though hibernation tides him over the worst. The warmer altitudes below seem to be as adverse to his welfare as the alpine zones are to the ground squirrels of the foothills, making the Belding the true squirrel of the summits.

One of his biggest homes in the High Sierra is McClure Meadow in Evolution Valley, 9,500 feet above sea level. This lush grassy flat is about one mile long and three-eighths of a mile wide. Like most Sierra meadows it was once a lake and around its ancient shoreline lodgepole pines grow thickly on old glacial moraines and among the scattered avalanche detritus that has tumbled from the spurs and ridges above. Evolution Creek meanders placidly down the middle; deer come to drink and fat trout splash after insects that fall on the water. During July and August blue-grey smoke from campfires puffs lazily into the nippy air and the smell of bacon and coffee often pricks at your nose. Overhead a Clark's nutcracker flaps leisurely along, his harsh caw knifing through the quiet Sierra air.

It's here that we find the Belding and his burrow system, which is dug into the soft brown loam of the meadow. There he stands regarding us, erect and rigid, his four-clawed hands held close to his chest like a nervous prizefighter waiting for the bell. Now he hurries off to see a friend and runs with his tail down, in a kind of awkward gait, clumsy and slow, like a short-legged dog. Instead of parting the stalks as he runs through the grass

he propells himself by a series of jumps, each taking him above the level of the grass so he can watch about him for such enemies as weasels, hawks, and coyotes.

Campers sometimes drive stakes into a meadow from which they tether pack stock. These pickets are often left in the ground and from a distance exactly resemble a Belding standing up and looking about—so much so that the Belding has earned the nickname "picket pin."

It's probably just as well that Beldings are a little frightened of people for bubonic plague is endemic in the fleas which live deep in their fur.

Our squirrel friend was named after Lyman Belding, a naturalist who lived in the San Joaquin Valley. Belding collected a specimen in Placer County in 1885 and sent it to Dr. C. Hart Merriam who subsequently named it *Spermophilus beldingi.*

The Belding feeds largely on grass stems and blades and sometimes can be seen pulling down grass heads to get the seeds. He is very fond of barley and oatmeal and delights in sneaking around the kitchen area of a party of campers. He seems to eat only for his immediate needs, his small cheek pouches holding scarcely an extra mouthful, and I have never seen him dragging food to his home or hiding it the way, say, Ohio squirrels do. His underground home has several entrances and he often goes in one way and out another. One afternoon I saw a friend chase a Belding down a hole and sit waiting for him to come out while the squirrel, emerging from another passage, crept up behind my friend and startled him with a loud rascally whistle and appeared to enjoy the joke immensely. A zoologist who dug into a burrow system in a wet meadow found the holes only 13 inches deep but the total length of the single system including blind branches (which probably went deeper as the meadow dried out) measured 54 feet.

The young, five or six in number, are born in late June. They stay close to their burrow and when alarmed dive pellmell into the hole. Near Colby Meadow in July I watched six half-grown youngsters scamper for their burrow with such gusto that one little fellow was pushed out of the way and dived instead into the ground. He got up dazed, staggering like a drunken sailor.

Beldings become quite fat in the early fall and hibernate regularly but the dates vary. Sometimes you see them running over patches of snow in early June. They have been reported as late as October 7th near Ten Lakes in Yosemite.

One day in Hutchinson Meadow I saw a Belding scamper under a rock. The rock was isolated on a large granite surface and I thought it a good place for a photograph because there wouldn't be a burrow in the granite. I uncased my camera, got down on my knees, and waited. No Belding. I double-checked the light reading and re-focussed my lens. Still no Belding. I knew he was under the rock. I waited. I looked at my watch. Then I happened to glance around to my left. There he was standing watching *me* with a mocking look on his face. There was no telling how long he had been there. "Which of us is the greater fool?" he seemed to say. "Are you observing my world or am I observing yours?"

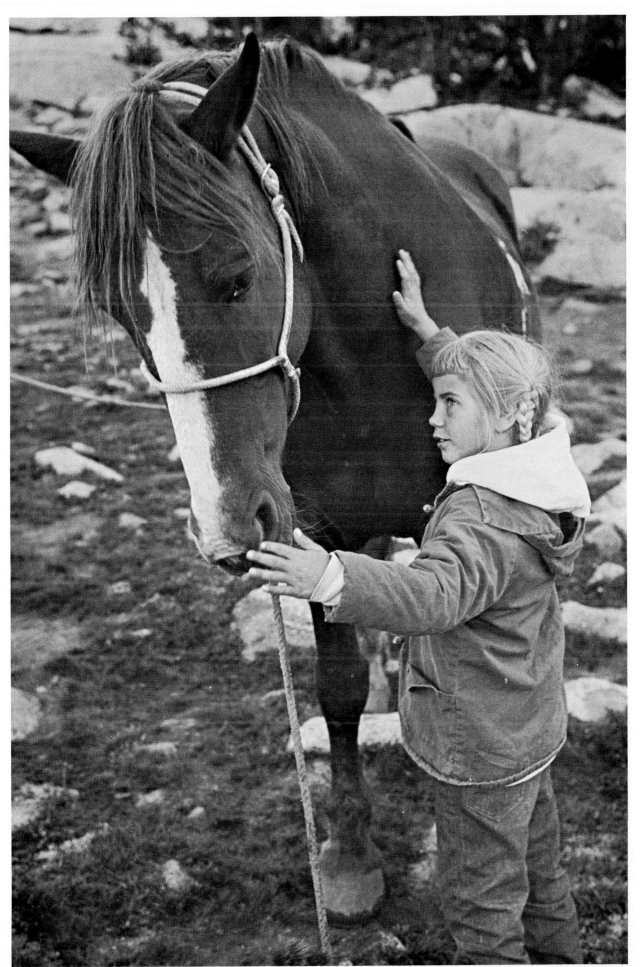

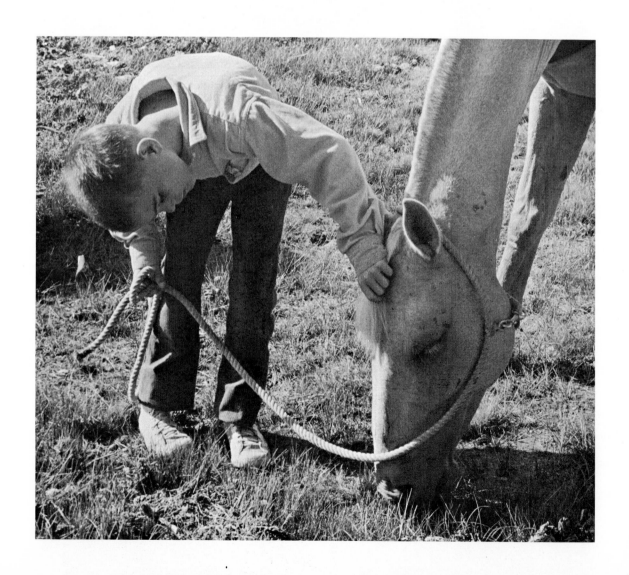

. . . and animals
and children

24

SILVER PASS TO MUIR PASS
The Packing Business

Every summer about 1,500 horses, mules, and burros haul supplies and people in the Sierra Nevada between Yosemite and Mt. Whitney.[1] The animals are owned by some 25 pack stations, about two-thirds of which are on the east side of the range. These pack stations are remakable enterprises which haven't changed their operations one bit in more than two generations. If you compare a photograph of a Sierra packer and his string of mules taken in 1905 or 1910 with one made today, the men and their equipment appear identical.

The man in the picture is tall and lean with a bronzed face that is squinting distrustfully toward the camera. He has on weary old Levi pants, stout boots with jingling spurs, a flannel shirt with a loop string from a pouch of Bull Durham tobacco dangling from one breast pocket, and his head is crowned with a well-used, wide-brimmed hat. (Old Sierra packers laugh at young horse wranglers who wear chaps which are designed for use in heavy brush, not the open trails of the High Sierra.) When the packer walks he limps from an old mule kick, and his hands and fingers are scarred and cracked from years of horseshoeing, running fences, riveting harness straps, and working with animals. He holds his reins easily in his left hand and the lead rope from the first of the five following mules in his right.

The packer tends to be curt with strangers and with the exception of "hello" or "good morning" never volunteers any information, just drilling you dead with dirty looks if you seem suspicious. He tends to scorn tenderfoot riders until they're his customers, then he can't help enough. He's fearless and merely annoyed by a washed-out trail, a tree across the way, or a snow-blocked pass, if there's the slightest chance of getting through. When he's not in a hurry you can't rush him no matter what you say. (If you get his dander up he's just liable to take off for the whole day.)

The packer is honest and can be trusted completely. He'll deliver mail with absolute reliability though an airmail letter may sometimes get a crumpled-up ride in a hip pocket for a month. When you get to know this taciturn, sometimes sullen individual you find he's not withdrawn and sour at all but—like a Vermont farmer—merely keeps to himself. If you ask him specific questions about this trail or that mountain, knowledge about which he's an authority, he begins to open up and you soon find out that he knows what he says.

The first day you nod at each other, the second day you speak a little, the third day you try a weak joke, the fourth you compare gripes against the government, and the fifth you inquire about his children and his winter job. If after a week you are finally asked, "What line of work do you follow?" you're accepted and have a friend for life!

The term packer refers to the man (there are a few women!) who takes parties in and out of the mountains and can perhaps be best described as a guide. He works for wages and sometimes a small share of the profits. The pack train operator, however, is the owner of the business and like proprietors everywhere he worries about the weather, lateness of snow melting, help, advertising, hay, advising people about trips, adequate corrals and supplies, writing letters, answering the telephone, trucks for hauling stock, and good relations with the park and forest services. In addition he has to face the major problem of the Sierra packing business: *everything happens in August.*

The packing season can be considered to be four months long with the animals actually working about 60 days. In July the meadows may be wet, the mosquitos bad, and some trails still covered with snow. Most people's vacations are timed to end with Labor Day in September. Some business comes again in October with the opening of deer season in national forests. (A substantial deer season packing business ended in 1940 when Kings Canyon National Park was created.) But in August most pack stations could rent out twice as many animals if they had them. One factor against expansion of services is the high investment in stock and gear. A second is the necessity of pasturing the animals eight months of the year when they earn nothing. A third is that expansion would be even harder on the Sierra grasslands which some forest and park service packing permits recognize by limiting numbers of stock.[2]

The 1965 rates for packing are about $6 a day for a horse or mule and $18 for a packer (including his horse). These daily rentals run to high figures quickly, a couple riding horses with a packer and two mules costs $294 a week, for example. Generally the rates are reduced slightly by offering each eighth day free or some other discount. But these prices begin to compare with the cost of foreign vacations and have discouraged some business. The amount of backpacking in the Sierra has perhaps doubled since 1950 while the packing business has declined slightly (except for the renting of burros which has sharply increased but has brought little dollar volume at $3 each per day).[3]

Pack stations are expensive places. Good Georgia or Tennessee mules are not only hard to get but are worth $200 apiece. Dude horses cost $150. The expenses of erecting and maintaining corrals and summer buildings are high. Since World War II the costs of barley, rope, horseshoes, and leather goods have quadrupled. Insurance and repairs on two or three trucks can easily top $1,000 a year, and an experienced packer draws $250-300 a month and keep.

Because the sums of money involved in running a packing business are large, inefficient operators have gradually been forced out. Each year there are two or three consolidations and the number of stations continues to drop. With the park and forest services concerned about the high mountain meadows, even more rules may be forced on the packers who now have to take in expensive hay under certain conditions. The packing business may unfortunately be pricing itself out of existence.[4]

I think the government agencies should do all they can to encourage the packing business in the Sierra. Some of the money spent for helicopters used for administrative purposes could well be directed to the pack stations late in the year when their business is slack and the meadows are dry. Packers are a highly individualistic group who sorely resent too many rules and regulations, and who especially rebel against being ordered around by young assistant rangers. Some control is necessary of course but diplomatic senior rangers among the park and forest services might work this out rather than the 21 or 22-year-old college graduates, "the brash worldbeaters" who are often sent to talk to men who have spent 20 or 30 or 40 years in the mountains and—though sometimes untutored—know and love every boulder and meadow, though they would rather die than admit it.

The packing business as practiced in the Sierra Nevada is unique. The Appalachians in the eastern United States have nothing comparable nor do the Alps in Europe (travelers from abroad are always amazed at pack stations). Packers and pack stations are an important part of the mountain scene in California and a way that someone not suited to hiking can ride a horse, meet a different breed of Americans, and find a sure trail to the wilds.

25

SILVER PASS TO MUIR PASS
The Highest Fountains

The mightiest rivers have the humblest beginnings. Here in a drop of icy water about to fall from a snowbank snug against a mountainside at Muir Pass is the start of the San Joaquin River, one of the largest streams of California. Of course it's difficult to point to a single spot and say "Here a river begins," for which tributary do you take? All you can do is to follow up the larger stream at each fork until you eventually come to a basin where the water from all sources collects together. Then you can point to a set of snowbanks and say, "Here, finally, is the beginning."

Muir Pass, 11,955 feet, is the dividing point between the South Fork of the San Joaquin and the Middle Fork of the Kings River. In the aerial view we look southwest across Helen Lake, the highest lake on the Middle Fork of the Kings. The final ridge climbing to Muir Pass rises above the lake and at its left end is the pass itself (if you look closely you can see a dot that is the stone shelter). On the far side of the ridge (to the extreme right) is the south half of Wanda Lake, the highest lake on Evolution Creek, the principal source of the South Fork of the San Joaquin. In the distance rises the black mass of Mt. Goddard, 13,568 feet high, first climbed by Lil A. Winchell and Louis W. Davis in 1879, and named by the Whitney Survey party in 1865 for George H. Goddard, a noted civil engineer and cartographer.

Once I accompanied half a dozen hikers to Muir Pass "to get the sunrise view." We were camped below Evolution Lake and planned to walk by the light of the moon which was then full. We got up at 2 a.m., gulped down some hot cocoa, and went slogging up the canyon. Unfortunately our plans to proceed by moonlight failed dismally, for as the canyon narrowed and the moon went down behind some mountain spurs we lost our light completely and found ourselves

stumbling about in the dark, trying to cross the inlet of Evolution Lake. It was too cold to poke along and we hustled to keep warm, our boot-prints sometimes leaving a path in the frost ice that covered the trail. Gradually the eastern sky brightened.

When we broke into the open area beyond Sapphire Lake the whole eastern sky was suffused with red. It was a wild and chilling scene: beautiful and savage. Never had I been in a place that felt so open and somehow so naked to the raw power of nature. I have always thought that that morning I was close to the earth of a million years ago: elemental and basic, with the brutal forces of ice and snow and water and wind somehow isolated and held together in that huge environment of bare, fundamental rock.

Aerial view of Muir Pass looking southwest. The black mass of Mt. Goddard (13,568) is at the upper right. Partially frozen Helen Lake is at the bottom; Wanda Lake is toward the center, right. Both lakes were named after Muir's daughters. The pass itself and the stone shelter (page 137) are at the left end of the ridge above Helen Lake. At the left is a close-up of a drop of water melting from a snowbank under the summit shadow of Mt. Goddard. These drops of water are the ultimate source of the South Fork of the San Joaquin River.

26

MUIR PASS TO PINCHOT PASS
Muir Hut

On top of Muir Pass stands the Muir Hut, a small stone shelter for travelers caught out during storms on this exposed section of trail. To the north the first campsite is at the lower end of Evolution Lake, 5.8 miles away. South the first appreciable timber is at Little Pete Meadow, 6.8 miles, making the hut the rough mid-point of a long, open stretch of trail. The views from Muir Pass are good, it's a fine stopping and resting place, and the hut is an ideal base for climbing Mt. Goddard or the Black Giant.

The little shelter fits its environment so perfectly that it's difficult to see it until you're almost there. The conical roof is made up of concentric circles of stone that decrease in diameter toward the top which resulted in a strong, maintenance-free roof, well able to withstand snow and violent winds. The hut—which all agree should last 1000 years—has benches and places for sleeping, a fireplace, candles, and a small stock of food and wood left by travelers through the years. Everyone crossing the pass is asked to bring a few sticks of wood for the emergency stockpile. One of the most interesting experiences at the hut is to read the summit register which contains the names of people who have crossed the pass together with their comments ("July 30, 1952: Balmy and warm. A very heaven on earth. Why didn't someone tell us there was a place like this 40 years ago?" "August 17, 1957: Boy Scout Troop 796 made the trip here from Darwin Bench in a record two hours and thirty minutes and if we hurry hope to . . ." "June 12, 1960: We made the pass at 11 a.m. after climbing through snow for two hours. The glaring whiteness is very hard on the eyes. A cold wind is blowing").

During 1929, George Frederick Schwartz, a professional forester whose home was in New York, wanted to sponsor a memorial to John Muir

and offered to contribute money toward the building of the John Muir Trail.

"Do something special with your money," suggested William E. Colby, then the secretary of the Sierra Club, "or else the money will be swallowed up in the state appropriations and you'll never know where it has gone.

"I suggested building a shelter on top of Muir Pass," recalled Colby, "and Schwartz agreed. I got the idea from an article in *National Geographic* magazine about an area down in the heel of Italy near Brindisi where there is practically no timber and very poor transportation. The people have to rely on stone and build these strange-looking but very practical and substantial huts. I worked out the size and drew the design from the pictures in the magazine and then turned it over to San Francisco architect Henry Gutterson who made regular drawings. A similar structure had been built on Longs Peak in Colorado and through correspondence we were able to get the results of the construction experience which was helpful.

"It was before the days of Kings Canyon National Park when Muir Pass was under the control of Sierra National Forest," said Colby. "The Forest Service very generously agreed to supervise the work which was dog-gone hard because of the location—about as difficult as you could find. M. A. Benedict was in charge of the forest and I recall that the foreman was Mike Wenz. The work was done in 1930.

"Since it was several miles above all timber, fuel as well as building materials had to be packed to the site on mules. All sand for mortar was packed nine miles, and during the last of the season even water had to be packed a long distance. The trip from the end of the last road took four days and much of the time an alternate trip had to be made to bring fuel up from the nearest timber.

"It's not surprising that the packing costs were without precedent. The hut cost $5,810.48 which broke down as follows:

Stone masons and workmen	23.3%
Packing	51.6
Material	13.5
Food, equipment, and misc.	9.3
Medical and insurance	2.3

Barrier Rock

MIDDLE FORK OF THE KINGS RIVER

"Barrier Rock proved to be a very difficult piece of work. The rock laid in floors, tapering to a feather edge on the overhanging side, and when a tread was blasted out these floors would slide off. This was repeated several times before a tread was obtained that would hold, and a short pitch exceeding 20 per cent had to be used."

JOHN M. HUGHES
Foreman, Muir Trail
Construction Crew, 1917

27

MUIR PASS TO PINCHOT PASS
Middle Fork of the Kings River

There are three ways to travel on the John Muir Trail. The first is to walk and carry your food and equipment on your back. This is the simplest, cheapest, and hardest. Carrying 30 or 40 or 50 pounds is an arduous task, but when you have everything with you, you can stop when and where you like. Once you have your outfit—a pack frame, a down-filled sleeping bag, a couple of pots and pans, and a few personal items—you are set for years and years.

You are almost as free as a bird. You can travel singly or in groups, you can leave at a moment's notice, and you can take short cuts and knapsack routes. But this freedom has its price in that you have to work hard to carry your equipment at high altitudes where your breath comes short and the trails are steep. Unfortunately your pack weighs the most at the beginning of a trip when you are in the poorest condition. (You don't get the limbs and lungs of a giant until you've been out for several weeks.)

Since World War II we have seen such notable developments as baffled sleeping bags made of tough nylon fabric, carefully engineered magnesium pack frames, and dehydrated and vacuum dried foodstuffs. It's remarkable how much nourishment you can get from a pound of these special foods. However as good as they are (and expensive too!) it's important to run through your entire camping diet on a trial run basis at home before you leave. Theoretical meals sometimes don't work.

I remember meeting a doctor, his wife and son, and another man near Silver Pass several years ago. They had been backpacking for a week and planned to continue for another 15 days. The doctor held up a tiny package.

"This is our breakfast," he said proudly. "It only weighs 2¼ ounces." He pulled out another package from his pack. "This is our lunch," he continued. "It weighs 5½ ounces. And this is our supper," he said triumphantly, holding up a third silver-colored envelope. "It weighs 15 ounces."

The people in my party all marveled and we listened with attention as the doctor told us about vacuum-dried foods and recited all the vitamins, nutrients, and calories contained in his small packages. "I worked it all out in my office," he said, "and I am confident that I have found out the secret of featherweight backpacking."

A week later the doctor and his party happened to stop in our camp since we were going in the same general direction. We asked them if they would like to look over some food that we were going to pack out of the mountains and discard. There were a number of oranges on the verge of spoiling, a few dented cans of vegetables, some candy bars that had melted and gotten mixed up with nuts, and several half-full boxes of pancake mix.

I have never seen such looks of eagerness on any four people in my life. They fell on the food—orange peels flew in all directions—and devoured every scrap of the edible bits and reverently packed away the rest to their camp.

The story emphasizes what we all know: each person needs a certain amount of bulky, wholesome food in his diet, and pills—no matter how fancy—don't have it. In the city you may eat three small meals; carrying heavy loads many miles on steep trails can easily double your appetite.

The second way to travel is to lead a burro, a mule, or a horse to carry your gear. This way you can take all your backpacking equipment, more personal items (cameras, books, binoculars), and have a little better diet. But now you need to worry about food for the animal which means you must plan to camp in locations where the stock will have ample grass. This is not simple with some Sierra meadows closed to grazing and the Park and Forest Services nervously watching other meadows. In addition you have to find the animal in the morning; sometimes a mule can wander for miles. A third point is that the mule or horse is fairly expensive and may need to be shod, obliging you to carry horseshoes, nails, a rasp, and a shoeing hammer. A burro doesn't wear horseshoes but this small animal can't carry much. If you lead pack animals you will spend at least two or three hours every day looking for them, packing and unpacking them, and worrying about their food and shoes. However once on the trail you can look around and enjoy the scenery without carrying a heavy burden.

The most deluxe way to travel is to have a packer take your equipment on mules and for you to ride a horse. This is expensive, but you can sit on your animal and look about you without ever thinking of the trail. The packer takes care of the animals, worries about their food, and deals with all the packing problems.

There are several notable variations of trail traveling. One is to be spot camped. In this scheme you have a packer take you to a location worked out in advance—often a beautiful remote place—and leave you and your equipment for a week or two after which he comes in for you with animals. A more spartan variation is for the packer to leave caches of food at specified places for a backpacker. (The directions for these locations are critical. There are *two* Junction Meadows. Once I spent days looking for food cached ". . . near a big gray granite rock just up from the trail near a kind of creek.") A very satisfactory back country plan practiced by guide Joe Wampler and on certain Sierra Club trips is to walk and have packers move the camp and duffel every day or two. With a group of 10 or 20 and a good leader this scheme becomes cheap and efficient. All an individual needs to carry is his lunch.

There is an axiom about mountain travel: the more you carry the less you see. Or as a mathematician might state it: the aesthetic perception of the bearer diminishes as the square of his increasing load. John Muir made almost legendary trips with nothing but a little tea and a sack of bread. Perhaps he was right. After all he saw the most and carried least.

28

MUIR PASS TO PINCHOT PASS
Grouse Meadow

The lush green meadows below timberline are among the most pleasant parts of the Sierra. Not only are they centers of camping and pack stock grazing but the open sunny glades are good places to see deer, squirrels, weasels, pine martens, and many birds. Conditions of moisture vary considerably and here you find the widest variety of wildflowers and grasses. Camping is excellent for you can choose any degree of sun or forest by working back from the edge of the meadow. Water is easy to reach, the campsite is protected from the weather, and firewood is usually prevalent. Meadows are often found near the junctions of canyons and are the crossroads of many trails. Finally, the scenic beauty is superb. Lovely foregrounds of grasses, water, and flowers lead smoothly into fine backgrounds of mountains and sky.

These meadows are mostly above 7,500 feet and are essentially basins where obstructions to drainage have caused large amounts of silt, sand, gravel, loam, and organic matter to accumulate. Without exception their defining characteristic is *wetness*, for the water table is too high to allow the growth of forest trees. Under natural conditions the border between forest and meadow is quite rigidly fixed and there is little encroachment of trees upon the meadow.[1] In Giant Forest in Sequoia National Park for example, the meadows are bordered with a dense growth of Sequoias and white firs. The Sequoias are 1,000 years old, yet have shown no tendency to advance upon the meadow.

The grasses and sedges in mature meadows reach a stable climax condition with their roots forming tough interlocking structures that mechanically impede tree growth. As long as the meadow sod is not heavily trampled, nor dried out by overgrazing, the meadow will remain green and healthy.[2]

Though careful studies by prominent scientists have shown that alpine meadows thrive for centuries, the story of these mountain grasslands during the past 60 years has been one of continuing decline. Investigations based on tree ring counts of invading conifers, photographs, and other data clearly indict overgrazing as the chief enemy of meadow land. In Sand and Mitchell Meadows on the South Fork of the Kaweah River for example, the boundary between grass and trees is well stabilized and has existed for hundreds of years. However just inside the old growth of bordering lodgepoles is a new growth of small pines about 150 feet in depth. When samples of these trees were cut in 1958 they were found to be 58 years old which exactly matched extremely heavy cattle grazing in 1900.[3]

The pattern of meadow destruction is always the same. Trampling and excess grazing beat down the grasses and sedges. Rough annual weeds, brush, and forest trees begin to replace the once-tall perennial grasses. Extended animal use kills many grass roots completely, leaving bare patches and dust wallows. Water begins to erode and to cut channels in the underlying silt, sand, and gravel, and the sinking water table lets the remaining grass dry out and die. Stream trenches widen, the banks cave in, soil washes away, and the trampled sand is exposed to wind. Catastrophic erosion finally kills the meadow completely.

Some prime Sierra meadows have been lost forever; others are in intermediate stages of deterioration; still others—mainly in isolated places—are in good condition. Many meadows on heavily traveled routes show invasions by lodgepole pines and rough weeds such as corn lilies, sure signs that drastic changes have taken place in the ecologic balance of the grasslands. If the meadow thus invaded is closed to grazing or the amount of grazing is controlled, the grass will tend to restore itself in five or ten years, depending on the severity of damage. Check dams, erosion gully plugs, and protective fencing may be needed. But if the water table has been permanently lowered, the meadow sod cannot regain the upper hand and the meadow will ultimately be lost to forest. The amount of overuse by grazing animals is directly related to forest invasion which varies from 50 feet in 50 years to as much as 100 feet in 12 years.[4]

It shouldn't be inferred from this discussion that all grazing is bad. Moderate use of meadows by pack stock is harmless and seems a legitimate function of the back country. The trouble is that certain camps are favored and nearby meadows get too much pressure. The practice of tethering burros is not good because their handlers tend to use the same pickets which results in circles of severely browsed and trampled grass. Animals are sometimes turned loose on meadows still wet from spring flooding.

Many packers recognize the grazing problems and go to considerable trouble to take their horses and mules away to healthy grass, which incidentally suits the animals better. Trails were once led *through* meadows; now they are routed *around* to keep the animals from turning boggy places into quagmires of mud and cut sod which later dry out and erode.

The Forest Service recognizes that recreation and water production—fortunately non-conflicting —are the primary functions of the High Sierra. National forest grazing permits for cattle on lower meadows are now closely tied to what the grasslands can reasonably support. The demand for commercial cattle handling in mountain areas has declined in recent years because of high trucking and management costs and the development of cheaper feeding schemes.[5]

✓   ✓   ✓

Grouse Meadow is a large wet meadow of about 50 acres that lies at an elevation of 8,300 feet on the Middle Fork of the Kings River just above Palisade Creek. It's a popular stopping place for parties coming south from Muir Pass who want to rest a day or two before tackling Palisade Creek and Mather Pass. In the early summer much of

the meadow is flooded, and coarse, tough-leaved sedges flourish in the marshier parts. In the drier places at the upper and lower ends of the meadow the varieties of sedges are finer and some grasses grow and of course these areas receive most of the grazing. Ecological studies in 1940 and again in 1958 showed that the meadow was in fair condition but some over-grazing had caused minor streambank erosion, small dry flats, and invasions of corn lilies and lodgepole pines at the upper and lower ends.[6]

The relationship between overgrazing and invasion by corn lilies is unquestionable. In Grouse Meadow however, invasions by lodgepole pines are indirect. In his 1958 study Dr. Carl Sharsmith pointed out that meadow soil is normally neutral in acidity. As overgrazing lowers the water table the soil dries out and becomes increasingly acidic which encourages a plant called westernbog blueberry which thrives in acid soil. This plant directly prepares the way for lodgepole pine growth by acting as a kind of seedbed nursery, accumulating leaf mold, litter and humus. In Grouse Meadow, lodgepoles grow up only from thickets of this shrub. Out in the drier parts of the meadow where overgrazing has occurred you will find dozens of yards of corn lilies and you will see lodgepoles growing directly from low thickets of westernbog blueberry.

✓   ✓   ✓

One surprising resident of marshy spots in Grouse Meadow is the sundew, a small plant that eats insects. It bears a pretty, five-petaled white flower at the end of a six-inch stalk. The flat leaves occur lower down and are about one-half inch long and spread around the stalk of the plant on long petioles. Scores of hairlike, red-tipped tentacles reach up from each leaf for one-eighth of an inch or so. Each tentacle has a drop of clear sticky fluid at its end. If a fly or other small insect comes in contact with one of these drops, the taffy-like fluid holds it fast. The more the insect struggles the more sticky drops it touches. The plant secretes digestive juices over its tiny victim and then absorbs nutrients from its body. A few days later the insect is gone. All of this happens on a scale so small you would probably never see it if it weren't pointed out.[7]

GROUSE MEADOW

Aerial view looking east at the Golden Staircase, the last and perhaps most difficult bit of construction of the John Muir Trail. Palisade Creek is at the right and here is practically a 'waterfall,' giving some idea of the steepness of the terrain. The white line (much wider and smoother than the actual path) indicates the trail which here is a masterpiece of construction, cleverly winding back and forth to minimize the grade. The staircase is a good pull with a heavy pack but taken slowly and steadily is not too long. Several serious accidents have occurred here with pack stock when packers have attempted to take the switchbacks too fast, with the result that the end mules have been pulled sideways across a switchback and spilled, dragging down the whole train. Experienced packers take such trails very slowly (to give the last mules time to get around the switchbacks) and always hold the lead rope in their hands, rather than tying it to their saddles.

29

MUIR PASS TO PINCHOT PASS
Golden Staircase

Before the trail was built up Palisade Creek and over Mather Pass, travelers had to detour a long distance west and south from the crest, going down the Middle Fork of the Kings River to Simpson Meadow, climbing over Granite Pass, dropping to the South Fork of the Kings, and ascending Paradise Valley back to the John Muir Trail, a detour of almost 50 miles from the highest peaks.

The first animal crossing of what is now known as Mather Pass, the direct route between the Middle and South Forks of the Kings, was made in 1897 by a sheepherder named Escallier who was caught by snow in November and somehow got his burro up the cliff at the head of Palisade Creek and over the divide.[1] Eleven years later the Le Conte party pronounced the pass feasible, but were entirely defeated when they tried to get their mules out of the canyon of Palisade Creek. "We again scouted about for a possible route," wrote J. S. Hutchinson. "There were several chutes leading down [the thousand foot wall], but they were choked with huge blocks fallen from the cliffs."[2]

In 1921, Robert Barrett of Cornish, New Hampshire, approached the hazardous cliffs from above while leading a group of Boy Scouts with 20 burros. The resourceful Barrett, a large, tall man with a long flowing beard, in a demonstration perhaps not seen since the days when the Forty-Niners crossed Donner Pass, got his burros down the cliff by lowering each one on a block and tackle.[3]

Later the same month the Hamlin party crossed the divide, named it after Stephen Mather, the first director of the National Park Service, and managed to get down the terrible cliff. Francis Farquhar and a friend followed their tracks on foot. "As we went back over their route we admired their energy and persistence, as well as the skill of their packers . . ." wrote Farquhar, "they had actually built a trail over that pass with their own hands."[4]

In July, 1922, J. S. Hutchinson took another pack party across Mather Pass and down the great cliff. "Gravity is of great assistance," he noted, thrilled to get to the bottom. "No one as yet, so far as we know, has been up Palisade Creek with a pack-train. Some day, however—soon, I hope—there will be a good trail through."[5]

Hutchinson's wish was not fulfilled until 1938, when the last link of the John Muir Trail was completed. Trail crews from Inyo, Sierra, and Sequoia National Forests blasted dozens of huge boulders from the cliff and patiently chinked and fitted together thousands of small rocks to make a first class route up the formidable cliff that has come to be known as the Golden Staircase.

30

MUIR PASS TO PINCHOT PASS
Erratics and Dike

During the formation of the Sierra, molten granite pushed to the surface from deep within the earth. When it reached the air it began to solidify and cool rapidly, though still molten underneath. As the granite cooled it contracted and surface tensions set up considerable stresses. In some places the strains on the rock increased until great cracks appeared and when these cracks reached the interior, molten rock flowed out again. Because of differences in cooling, however, fractional crystallization occurred and slightly different kinds of granite often came to the surface. Since the crystalline structure varied, some granites were harder and more resistant to weathering. In this case we see a whitish, fine-grained granite called aplite which is relatively hard. Sometimes the granite alongside it weathers away an inch or two, leaving a tiny wall or dike standing above the rest of the rock.

If you look closely you will see several tear-drop-shaped bits of rock an inch or two long on the surface of the granite at the right. These are called xenoliths and show that sedimentary or volcanic rocks were present when the molten granite arose. The xenoliths were formed when bits of the then-existing rock fell into the molten granite and were recrystallized. Xenoliths always tell the geologist that older rock existed.

When the world of smoke and fire ended, the slow process of weathering commenced. Water seeped into tiny cracks and in aeons of time forced some of them open. We can see by the glacial polish on top of the granite that during the Ice Age the glaciers flowed from left to right and smoothed and rounded the hard rock. Cracks have continued to develop and the granite is very slowly breaking into smaller pieces. We can get an idea of the slowness of the weathering by looking at the polished surface left by the glaciers which ran across this granite from 11,000 to 30,000 years ago. In all that time only some of the burnished surface—a fraction of an inch thick to begin with —has weathered away.

The three boulders on top of the rock are called erratics and were left when the glacier melted. Sometimes these boulders are of quite different material and color, and can be traced back to distant mountains and help chart the course of ancient ice flows. A few grasses, one small shrub, and a white-barked pine are growing around the rock and some of their roots will gradually push apart cracks in the granite or hold water which will do the same job. Eventually lichens will grow on the surface of the granite and will help break the hard rock into grains of soil which one day will flow down the mountainside on their way to the sea.

(Right.) Granite formation southeast of lower Palisade Lake. We are in the open rock area of the high country and look eastward toward the Sierra Crest and Mt. Bolton Brown.

Corn Lily

Mather Pass and the Palisades
from the South

MATHER PASS

31

PINCHOT PASS TO GLEN PASS
Wilderness Guide

Joe Wampler has been taking people into the wilds of the Sierra Nevada along the John Muir Trail since 1950. From June until early September he guides both the inexperienced who want to see the country for the first time and the experienced who want to travel without bothering with packing and cooking. People new to the back country generally need guidance in selecting boots and sleeping bags and arranging their hiking or riding schedules. Joe has plenty of savvy in these matters, having safely guided several thousand people ranging in age from 8 to 79.

He takes 12 to 25 people at a time, with sufficient packers and animals to transport 30 pounds of duffel for each person plus the general camp equipment which includes a sizable first aid chest and even a tiny library. Joe has a cook, a second cook, and a college-age helper or two to assist with his camp. Toilet and bath tents are erected, the kitchen is set up near a stream, and the people put their ground sheets and sleeping bags around the camping area, most selecting private sites open to the sun and the view. Rain is infrequent in the Sierra during the summer and few use tents, relying instead on canvas tarpaulins which can be rigged over their campsites in case of a rain shower. Joe's only rules are no solo peak climbing and "please wash downstream from the kitchen."

"I give people good hot food and plenty of it," says Joe, "get them started early in the morning in this beautiful John Muir country, and they are pretty generally enthusiastic about the area and my trips. I'm proud that most of my guests have come because their friends have liked my trips and recommended me."

The majority of people on Joe's trips walk but a few ride horses and there are always a few spare horses along in case of sickness, a sprained ankle, or an acute set of blisters. During the trip the whole camp moves from place to place, generally 8 to 12 miles, with each third or fourth day a layover or day of rest. This gives the fishermen, photographers, bird watchers, and amateur geologists plenty of time to enjoy their hobbies. Usually the trips are scheduled for two-week periods, and start and finish at side trails that connect with road-ends.

Like good guides and teachers everywhere, Joe actually leads his people very little. He prefers to suggest and tell about the way and then to step back and let his guests experience the newness and the discovery themselves. Most of the people hike or ride at widely separate intervals in groups of two or three. Joe is always in the background somewhere and he tries to keep an eye on everyone—especially during the first few days when city-soft hikers occasionally overexert themselves. People sometimes drive all night to commence a trip; a long hike at high altitude the following day can cause sickness and nausea. Joe tries to minimize this by suggesting that his arriving guests get adequate sleep the night before and then hike slowly and steadily. He believes that hikers should eat small amounts of food and hard candy at frequent intervals.

But if someone gets sick Joe nurses him with care and genuine concern. He dispenses a few pills, brings hot tea and crackers, and kneels by his patient's sleeping bag to cheer him with a few reassuring words.

This is not hard for Joe is a good talker. He is well read and is delighted to discuss conservation, disarmament, bighorn sheep, the study of Arabic, or U. S. foreign policy. In fact once he's begun it's hard to restrain him whether the subject is climbing Milestone Mountain or the problem of radicals in the Republican party.

Each morning at 5:30 or 6:00 a.m. Joe rouses the camp with a series of tremendous yodels that echo back and forth among the canyons. Everyone gets up, arranges his duffel, and leaves it for the packers. He then eats a substantial hot breakfast which the staff has prepared, and hits the trail for the next camp, usually getting under way by 6:30 or 7:00 a.m. In spite of a few grumbles the first week, the campers soon appreciate the wisdom of early rising. You hike in the cool of morning, you can stop along the trail at a stream or lake to soak your feet or cast for a fish, and after a lazy lunch at the top of a pass or at a flower-filled meadow, you get to the next camp by early afternoon.

Joe Wampler was born in Timberville, Virginia, one of five children. He attended Bridgewater College in his home state and later the University of California in Berkeley where he majored in anthropology. He won his master's degree at the Pacific School of Religion under Dr. William Frederic Badé, the noted archaelogist. He became Dr. Badé's assistant and went on research expeditions in Palestine in 1929, 1932, and 1935. Appointed curator of the Palestine Institute at the school, he continued with his studies and published an outstanding book on pottery. During World War II he was a first lieutenant in the U. S. Army Signal Corps.

After the war, discouraged by the unrest in the Middle East which made further archaeological expeditions into Palestine impossible, he left the field, and worked at various jobs for short periods. From 1946 through 1949 he went on Sierra Club summer mountain trips as a woodcutter and gradually began to think of taking small groups into the mountains on his own. At first he tried to promote a trip along the Pacific Crest Trail from Mexico to Canada but found few takers. Shortening his trip to the John Muir Trail in 1950 he began his present schedule of summer outings which have put his administrative talents to good use.

A vocal, fiercely independent, somewhat spare man, Joe keeps himself in superb physical condition by careful diet and a thousand miles or more of walking each year. He has been taking courses in wildlife management at the University of California and lacks but a few credits for a master's degree. Married in 1956, now divorced, he has a young son whom he looks forward to taking on his trips one day. During the rest of the year Joe runs wilderness trips in Arizona and Mexico from his headquarters in Berkeley.

The people who come on Joe's trips are generally drawn from professional categories. Doctors lead the list with lawyers, engineers, and teachers close behind, although a list of occupations would run from aviation mechanics to zookeepers. Many bring their families.

"One thing my people have in common after a trip is some feeling of the spiritual significance of the wilderness," says Joe. "I know this is difficult to talk about but just about everyone begins to feel some rumbles of a private mystical experience when they see a quiet mountain lake sparkling in the sun or the build-up of a towering cumulous cloud over a granite headland. It's something deep inside you, felt more than talked about, that makes you want to keep this land just as it is.

"The John Muir Trail country is my country. None of the other areas in which I lead trips have the scope or challenge of these mountains. Where else can you spend three or four weeks hiking in just *one* national park and camp among dozens of 13,000 and 14,000-foot peaks?

"I believe the wilderness is one of the last frontiers where a person can learn self reliance and independence," says Joe. "Americans were once lean and tough and could think for themselves. Now they want automatic automobiles, predigested thinking, and a government to lead them by the hand from the cradle to the grave. Do you think our forefathers ever had to worry about dieting? Certainly not! They went out and worked hard and made their own way. Nowadays too many Americans are what I call Fat Babylonians and want comfort and ease; not the challenge of the next mountain, the next pass, or the next crossing of the distant canyon."

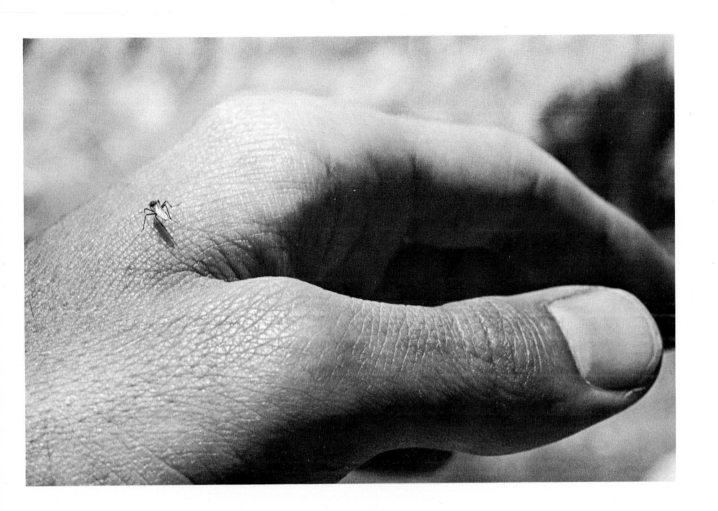

Mosquito

Each paradise has its plague, and the affliction of the early summertime High Sierra is the mosquito. Small, vicious, innumerable, obnoxious in all ways, these pests linger until the snowbanks have melted away and the marshy meadows have dried. Then mercifully they are suddenly gone. Most comments about mosquitos are wholly blasphemous — and should be. Once I heard an old packer who was fanning away a cloud of the whining pests from around his head cry out: "Why did God make mosquitos?"

South toward Pinchot Pass
from Upper Basin

Tired . . .

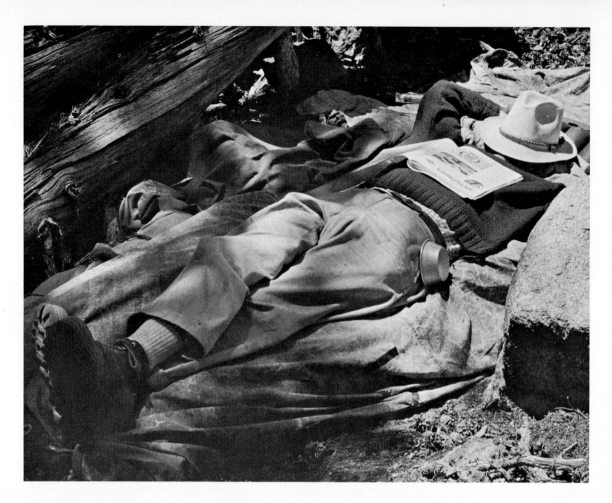

162

. . . so tired

Twin Lakes and Mt. Cedric Wright

The Spanish word *sierra* literally means *saw* and is used by the Spaniards to designate mountain ranges that are notched or cut like the teeth on the blade of a saw. The word *nevada* means snow covered. Sierra Nevada therefore means snowy mountain range with strong connotations of massiveness and jaggedness.

The California mountains known as the Sierra Nevada were first sighted, described, and mapped by the Franciscan missionaries Francisco Garcés and Pedro Font, who accompanied the Anza expedition that marched overland from Sonora, Mexico, in 1775-76, to found San Francisco.

On April 3, 1776, from a hill near the junction of the Sacramento and San Joaquin rivers, Font wrote: "If we looked to the east we saw on the other side of the plain at a distance of some thirty leagues a great *sierra nevada*, white from the summit to the skirts, running about from south-southeast to north-northwest."[1]

Francis Farquhar, an authority on Sierra history, has written: "The Sierra Nevada is distinctly a unit, both geographically and topographically, and is well described as '*una sierra nevada*.' Strictly speaking, therefore, we should never say 'Sierras,' or 'High Sierras' or 'Sierra Nevadas' in referring to it . . . for our part we rather like to keep in mind the unity of our great range by calling it simply 'The Sierra' or 'The Sierra Nevada'."[2]

166

32

PINCHOT PASS TO GLEN PASS
Woods Creek and Basalt Flow

About 1½ miles southwest of Twin Lakes. Woods Creek tumbles through an old flow of basalt that is a remarkable study in joint fracturing. As we have seen, a significant part of the disintegration of rock is due to naturally occurring cracks. Frost, heat, and water gradually open up these cracks over a very long time and the rock finally spreads and breaks. The greater the destructive force the faster and more extensive the splitting and wearing away. Here the falling water works constantly, eroding away grains of rock and slowly working upstream as the water wears away its bed.

This formation was part of an emergence of molten basalt that flowed across the canyon not long before the Ice Age. You can see how the top of the basalt flow was sheared off smoothly by the glaciers. Since that chilly time the water has gradually cut a small box canyon exactly following the vertical joints in the rock which here lean to the left toward the top. The vertical partings on the left are severely cracked in several places and one day more of the loosened rock will topple down as some of it has already. Note the two unweathered faces of rock on the right front where slabs of basalt have cracked off recently. One fair-sized lodgepole is firmly established on top along with a few shrubs, and their roots growing in the cracks add another force working to break up the basalt.

The incredible slowness of formation of the box canyon can be judged by the rocks at the top left which have been rounded to some extent by long exposure to the weather. In roughly 30,000 years the water has cut down about 30 feet or about one foot every ten centuries. Reduced further this works out to be one inch every 830 years or 1/1000 of an inch per year.

33

PINCHOT PASS TO GLEN PASS
Fin Dome and Rae Lakes

Most places in the High Sierra are named for people, incidents, or notable features. For people, for example, we have Glen Pass (Ranger Glen H. Crow), Mt. Lyell (Geologist Sir Charles Lyell), and Rose Lake (Painter Rosa Hooper). Incidents of the past are tied to Disappointment Peak, Hungry Packer Lake, and Hell For Sure Pass. Thousand Island Lake, Diamond Mesa, and Table Mountain directly describe features of the landscape.[1]

Fin Dome belongs to the last classification and was named by Bolton Coit Brown in 1899 when he compared the steep ridge west of Rae Lakes to a sea serpent and marked on his sketch map "The Head," "The Fin," and "The Tail." Only Fin Dome has survived on modern maps. It seems a good name, for the thumb-like dome projects 1,142 feet above the lakes and heralds their location for miles around.

The graceful pinnacle was roughed out of an enormous block of granite during aeons of time by exfoliation, the process mentioned earlier in which a dome casts off successive curving shells or scales from its outer surfaces, somewhat like the outer layers of an onion peel away. The dome was brought more into prominence by the later work of glaciers which swept northward from Sixty Lake Basin and the vicinity of Glen Pass. The ice covered most of the landscape but flowed completely around the unyielding dome which stood above the glaciers. It was sculpted into sharper relief when tons of nearby less-resistant rock were swept away and the shoulders of the dome were bared by the powerful ice. Geologists call such an island in moving ice a *nunatak*.[2]

We can see from the smoothed rock on the lower contours how high the ice came and speculate how the resistant granite must have parted the ice. Notice the erratic boulders left by the

melting ice on the lower shoulders of the dome. Today we can also see a well-developed avalanche slope on the east face of the north shoulder and some exfoliation on the southeast side.

Other action besides glacial ice has been at work on the dome, softening and smoothing its contours. The splintered appearance has been produced by frost which has split and cracked open the prominent vertical seams in the granite and caused the loosened blocks to tumble down. Some of the darkened patches on the rock are lichens, simple common plants that consist of fungus bodies combined with colonies of microscopic one-celled algae. As the lichens grow they produce acid strong enough to disintegrate the granite, helping the weathering process that eventually turns the rock into soil.[3]

In the photograph, taken from an airplane, we are looking southeast across Rae Lakes, principal source of Woods Creek, a main tributary of the South Fork of the Kings River. Though the date is July 12 we can still see ice in the upper lake. Nearby Dragon Lake, 11,120 feet, near the top of the photograph, is still frozen over. The Muir Trail goes along the lakes on the left and crosses to the right on the land bridge just below the ice where it begins a steep ascent to Glen Pass.

How barren the landscape seems from an elevation of several thousand feet! How smooth and freshly swept the ice has left the rock (it seems like only yesterday except for the trees). There is little soil for vegetation and even the few foxtail and whitebark pines are slow-growing and relatively small. The ice scooped out and transported away the less resistant material in the valley and water filled the depressions, making lakes like beads on a necklace, so-called paternoster lakes, typical glacial tarns.

FIN DOME AND RAE LAKES

34

PINCHOT PASS TO GLEN PASS
Polemonium

Above 11,000 feet along the southern part of the John Muir Trail you sometimes see delicate light blue flowers sticking up from dry rocky ridges near the highest passes. This is sky pilot or *Polemonium eximium,* the rarest and sturdiest of the 20 varieties of polemonium that grow in the United States.[1] It's a perennial plant with several or more eight-inch stems growing from the same root crown, each bearing a dense two-inch cluster of tiny flowers at its top. A group of such stems and their heads of showy flowers makes a fine mountain bouquet, certainly when growing in an unexpected place.

The plant seems to thrive under conditions of extreme temperature variations. During the summer the noon temperature is often 85 or 90° while at night it plunges to 20 or 30°. The stem and sticky leaves are covered with fine hairs which may help protect them from such extreme of heat and cold. The frail-looking stem is actually quite tough and fairly rigid for its length, which no doubt helps the plant survive the high winds of its alpine world. The smell of polemonium is musky and cloying and almost too sweet. Close-up it is unpleasant but farther away becomes quite distinctive. Sometimes you can find the plants by smell if you are nearby and downwind.

Polemonium shows up when the snow melts which usually occurs in late July or August above 11,000 feet. The plant bears its flowers quickly and doesn't waste any time. You feel that its summer life cycle is done at a run to beat the first storms of winter. Indeed you have to find polemonium on almost the right day or else its flowers will be spent. (I have always thought that the plant must have the metabolism of a humming bird to grow and flower so quickly.) Often when you stop to get your breath while going up the trail you will see the nodding heads of the bluish flowers sticking up all around you from the rocks, sometimes a hundred or more clusters growing wherever they can find a little gravel or crude soil to put down their tough and determined roots.

Fire in the Sky

Yes I sit by my campfire
And watch the red and yellow flames
Quicken the dry logs to ash.
The chill of the night scrapes at my back and as I turn to warm myself
I look to the ice-black world above.
There hangs the dome of the night sky
Twice as high as imagination
And three times as wide as common sense.
I hunt for a few starry friends but the names are strange
And my memory is wounded by the sight of so many.
How cold and far and noiseless seem the distant stars.
Are they mere pinpricks in the sky to let the lights of heaven through
Or is each a separate world with a song of its own? . . .

Who's up there?
Who's up there in those worlds so high?
Are there green men and blue men with three-sided eyes
And stripe-skinned young women who tiptoe and fly?
Do these creatures from elsewhere have friends and love life
And eat pickles, hate dentists, drink beer, and duck strife?
Do they tremble with wonder under their star-streakéd sky
And throw logs on their campfires and look up and sigh?
What's up there?
What's up there in those worlds so high?
Too far to cry out or to wave or to fly?

Yes I don't care how those other people look.
I don't care how their heads are shaped.
My question is simply
What do they feel in the essential parts
Down deep in their hearts?
Is someone next to his campfire in one of those worlds out there?
Is one of the winking lights I see from the fire at his feet?
Does the flickering rhythm of the stars
Come from the flickering flames of a million distant campfires? . . .
It's all too much to think about.
But I have
And now I'll always see a correspondence
Between the flickering stars and the fire at my feet.
Ah poor reasoning man and the quandaries you invent.
Now to bed
Enough of this dream.

35

GLEN PASS TO MT. WHITNEY
Back Country Ranger

During the summer months Ranger Dana Abell looks after fifty square miles of primitive country in Kings Canyon National Park. His territory is from Glen Pass south to Forester Pass along the John Muir Trail, east to Kearsarge Pass and Mt. Keith, and west to Junction Meadow, Charlotte Creek, and the Gardiner Basin. It's a wild up and down land with many 12,000 and 13,000 foot peaks, plenty of steep and scary canyons but well sprinkled with quiet lakes, alpine forests, and peaceful meadows. Some of Dana's remote canyons are seldom disturbed by people, but other lakes and valleys and meadows are fished and camped and grazed almost to death. Even in the back country it seems that everyone goes where everyone else goes. Kearsarge Pass is the main access trail from the east and the route most of Dana's customers take. It's his job to keep camping and grazing under a measure of control and to tell people about the grand national park they're in.

"You'd be surprised how many people I meet who don't even realize they are in a park," said Dana as we sat on a big rock at Bullfrog Lake. "Some are fishermen with their eyes so glazed with thoughts of trout they never look up from their poles. Others are hikers with their heads down who are determined to walk 100 miles. When I tell them where they are they usually begin to look around a little and I try to pass on a fact or two about the mountains—enough to get them asking questions and pausing to look around on their own. For instance I met two fellows and a girl in their twenties about an hour ago. I happened to comment about the reddish cones on some low-lying, almost prostrate white-bark pines nearby. I told the three backpackers—on their first trip—about these weather-stunted trees and explained how frost kept killing off any branches that rose much above the rest of the plant. I showed them

how the flexible branches bent with the winds and how they could lie flat under the crushing snows of winter, and so forth, and got these people to realize that here were live and thriving pines, no longer unknown shrubs. I like to think that those people will recognize a *Pinus albicaulis* in the future."

Dana is the sole representative of the National Park Service in his territory. "I am here to let people know that someone cares about the country," he said. He looks after the campgrounds, does minor trail maintenance, keeps trail registers in order, supervises grazing, and is on hand in case someone breaks a leg or gets seriously ill. He has a small FM portable radio and each day he calls park headquarters. The week before he had had a radio request to find a backpacker whose father had died and whose presence was urgently needed.

I asked Dana about numbers of travelers and how he went about his business.

"Last Saturday—August 3rd—was fairly typical," he said. "There were about 200 people camped between Kearsarge Pass and Charlotte Lake. Some were just passing through. Others were in for two or three days on up to two weeks or longer. There were about 25 parties in all—usually two to five in a group. In addition there was a Sierra Club burro party and a troop of Boy Scouts. Most of the people were backpackers. I would judge about 80 per cent carry their gear on their backs. I spent the day at Kearsarge Pass and talked to about 60 people."

According to Dana the biggest problems of the back country are camping litter and grazing. In 1960 there was a big clean-up at Bullfrog Lake and Vidette Meadows. Tons of cans and bottles were hauled out on mules. Now the attempt is to keep up with the cans and bottles by asking that parties with animals haul out everything they bring in

174

and that backpackers carefully flatten their cans and carry them out or leave them at designated places.

"Many new campers don't realize how a few cans and bottles from each party soon add up to tons of debris and ruined sites," said Dana. "In addition some people chop down the picturesque living trees around the campsites when there is plenty of down wood to be picked up just a little further away—often dry, pitchy, rotten, and easy to break up against a rock. The green trees cut down don't even burn of course so the campers' hard chopping efforts are a complete waste. The wood is no good for cooking, the camp is ringed by stumps that will be around for a hundred years, and a debris of green useless wood is left behind. Experienced campers seldom bring hatchets or axes. I make sure I tell people these things.

"Every camping group is required to have a fire permit which is issued free. However to get the permit you have to sign your name and address. We have noted an amazing improvement in camping manners since names and addresses have been required and kept on file.

"The second problem is grazing," continued Dana. A few key meadows in heavily camped and traveled areas have been so overgrazed that we have had to close them to all stock or else there wouldn't be any meadows at all—only washed out sandy flats. We reckon a meadow takes 12 to 20 years to recover if we catch it in time. We have noted a definite recovery in Vidette Meadow since it was closed to grazing in 1958."

Grazing control is sometimes a problem to enforce. When I saw Dana in 1963, he had just chased out the burros of a party which had picketed them on closed meadows in spite of very obvious signs.

Practically everyone Dana meets is anxious to cooperate when he explains that a major goal of the park is to keep the primitive back country as unsullied by man as possible so people of the future can enjoy it too. He issued only three citations in 1963. His main strength for enforcement purposes comes from his presence, his explanations, his uniform, and his badge. He carries no firearms and uses no pack stock, going everywhere on foot.

Dana lives in a small cabin at Charlotte Lake with his wife and three children, Larry (11), Einar (10), and Adis (6). Each morning he walks out somewhere in his district, occasionally taking one of the older boys with him. He is packed in on June 15th with 950 pounds of food and equipment, enough to last until Labor Day when he leaves for the season. Another ranger comes in for the month of September.

Dana and his wife and children love the summer life but admit that it's vigorous living. "It's glorious but we really are tired sometimes," said Mrs. Abell, who figures that she spends three days a week washing clothes. First the wood has to be collected to heat the water that has to be hauled. She also does a good deal of baking. ("No baking powder is needed at this altitude.") The rest of the time she hikes with the children. The family brings in a great deal of dried food which properly prepared is tasty and nourishing but they miss fresh fruit. I happened to notice one of Dana's sons eyeing an orange I had in my pack and casually asked whether he would like it. "*Would I!*" he answered, eagerly tearing off the thick skin.

Dana has a Ph.D. in zoology and is professor in charge of the park management curriculum at

Here are three young men carefully picking their way down the south side of Glen Pass. They left Rae Lakes at 7 a.m. and hoped to be at Bullfrog Lake by noon. But they got so excited by the view on top of the pass that they decided to take a few photographs. This necessitated unpacking one burro. After the pictures the young men decided they might as well have lunch (at 10 a.m.). The other burro balked at standing around and sat down. It took two hours to get the burros up and re-packed. Now the hikers hurry along, still miles from their destination. We see by the shadows that the time is early afternoon. Another day's plans shot . . .

Sacramento State College where he has pioneered an undergraduate school for the training of park and recreational specialists. He calls himself an ecologist, and says that park management is applied ecology. He is an expert at identifying plants and whips out a pocket magnifying glass at the first sign of any unusual leaves or flowers.

He was born in California, served in World War II, and attended the University of California. While at school he worked as a summer ranger at the Ash Mountain headquarters of the park.

When I talked with Dana the most surprising thing I found out was his incredibly low pay as a summer ranger. He draws a salary at a GS-4 rate—$960 for the season—slightly above a federal elevator operator, the same salary as many federally-employed gardeners, and well below what a truck driver hired by the U. S. makes. The job specification sheet for his position however covers almost an entire page and lists such diverse responsibilities as fire-fighting, lectures on natural history, law enforcement, first aid, participation in rescues, wildlife censuses, etc. Dana would consider coming permanently as a summer ranger if the pay were at the GS-7 level, certainly a reasonable wage.

In spite of the humiliation of the low pay, ("It's a good thing the season doesn't last longer or I couldn't afford to subsidize the job.") Dana likes his job as a summer ranger. Every year 300 to 400 men apply for the 45 summer ranger positions in the park. Twelve of the jobs are in the back country.

"What will camping be like here in ten years?" I asked.

"There is definitely money in future budgets to control camping more," he said. "We will establish regular campgrounds at the heavy pressure points and put out rangers to look after things. We envisage a kind of back country zoning for the future. There will be two general areas, heavy use places like Bullfrog and Rae Lakes where camping will be restricted to established sites. The other areas are primeval places like Center Basin or Baxter Lakes: fairly difficult to get to."

In the days I spent north of Forester Pass I came to know the familiar sight of Dana well, the round park service hat perched jauntily on his head and a long shovel over the shoulder of his clean but un-ironed shirt. He was always cutting drainage channels on sections of flooded trail or working in campgrounds, shoveling out old fireplaces or smashing tin cans and putting them in burlap sacks. The packers in the region secretly dreaded meeting him for though the trail greetings were cordial, Dana always managed to cajole them into hauling out a sack or two of flattened tin cans.

Ph.D.'s smashing tin cans! What next!

Signs
along the Trail . . .

... are milestones

180

in one's experience

36

GLEN PASS TO MT. WHITNEY
Bighorn Sheep

Without question one of the most aloof, independent, and hard-to-see residents of the Sierra Nevada is the bighorn sheep. This champion of the crags, who thrives in what seems an impossible environment, truly has the respect of all mountaineers. Details of his life are sketchy but what is known of his mountain home and manner of living are unusual enough to attract and excite almost anyone.

The bighorn is roughly the size of a domestic sheep though there all resemblance ends, for while the bighorn is fleet of foot and a fearless wonder when it comes to climbing, his domesticated cousin is cowardly, dull, unthinking, and relatively lifeless. An adult bighorn ram stands 30 to 40 inches high at the shoulder, in general is slim and muscular, and except when molting in the spring, has a uniform dark sandy brown coat with 'a light rump patch and light muzzle. Ewes and lambs are generally paler. On some sheep the rump patch is bisected by a dark dorsel stripe. The tail is dark. Weights run from 150 pounds for a three-year-old ewe to 200 pounds for mature rams.[1]

The hooves are long, narrow, and hollow cupped. The rear part has rounded, rubber-like tissue that grips well on rock. Each half of the hoof can move independently from the other which allows the foot to work fully on either flat or irregular surfaces. The front feet of the bighorn are larger than the rear which helps when sorting out their tracks from those of deer.

The great horns of the male bighorn are the crowning glory of the species, frequently spreading to 24 inches and measuring 16 inches in circumference where they leave the head. The horns are not shed but continue to grow year after year. They begin to appear on the lambs at three months. Those of the rams are thicker and diverge outward while the horns of the ewes are smaller,

more goat-like, and grow almost parallel to each other. During the first year the ram curl becomes evident and growth continues rapidly at the base of the horns, each increment being added something like the annual growth rings of a tree (you can calculate a ram's age by counting these segments). The amount of growth decreases after six or seven years and by the time the ram reaches the age of 12 or 14, the yearly growth adds only a diminishing wrinkle at the base of the horns which by this time are massive and approach a full circle when viewed from the side. A measurement around the outside circumference of each horn may approach a yard at this time. A skull and horns often weigh 30 pounds.[2] Because of this mass, the horns may act as a counterweight, like the balancing pole of an acrobat, explaining the erect carriage of the head which seems to float as the animal bounds away up a steep slope.[3]

In the Sierra the mating season is in the autumn. When the ewes come in heat the rams literally come on the run. As many as eleven rams have been seen chasing one ewe, though the number is usually far less.[4] The younger females lead the rams on a merry chase sometimes leaping on narrow ledges with enough room for only one animal. The older ewes submit more readily to the rams who not bothering to look where they are going, sometimes stumble and fall during their strenuous chases.[5]

Fighting between rams is much publicized but little understood. Ralph and Florence Welles, by far the most experienced observers of bighorn, wrote in 1961:

Certainly [fighting] has nothing to do with the premating collection and maintenance of a "harem" or ewe herd; nor does it seem to result in the elimination of one ram from participation in mating activity with a certain ewe. From our ob-

servations, the "fight," "joust," "contest," "clonking," or "brain busting" appears to have no objective whatever except the satisfaction of some deep-seated urge aroused by the mating instinct and demanding and receiving an outlet for its own sake.[6]

A fight follows a definite pattern. Two rams mill about one another, sometimes for hours while they blow, growl, and groan. Each pretends to be disinterested and may turn away to eat or polish his horns on a bush but while doing so he carefully watches the other. Sometimes the rams strike or bump each other, often in the genitals, but this seems to be part of the preliminary jousting and appears to cause no discomfort. Occasionally both rams rear and lunge directly but the usual procedure is to walk away from each other a certain number of paces—like two cowboys in a western movie—whirl, rise to their hindlegs, sight down their noses at one another, and charge. Their great horns meet head on with tremendous force, estimated by the Welles at 50 to 70 miles per hour

and the equivalent of a 2,400 pound blow. The rams always synchronize their movements so they hit perfectly head on. If one tilts his head to the left, the other ram tilts his head to match. As many as 40 massive blows have been counted during an afternoon, the sound of the encounter clearly carrying three-quarters of a mile. The front sections of the horns are frequently heavily scarred from such fighting.

Lambs are born in May or June. The ewe isolates herself for the birth and leaves her offspring —usually one—hidden among the rocks while she rejoins the herd for short periods, alternating between her lamb and the band for a week or two until the youngster is strong enough to follow the adults. Growth is rapid the first summer and at 3½ months—when they cease serious nursing—the lambs are one-half the size of their mothers. The young sheep are frisky and delight in running, jumping, and hopping about. Often several stand with their heads together and push at one another. When the mother moves to a new place the lamb follows, usually climbing up and down every rock on the way, like a child stepping through mud puddles, rather than going around the obstacles as do the adults.

The senses of hearing and smell appear normal in the bighorn. Their vision is superb. "While watching a band of eight [sheep] about 1½ miles away through 12x glasses," noted one account, "we determined by repeated trials that they could see a wave of the hand although they were barely visible to the naked eye."[7] The sheep tend to run in small bands of 5 to 15 individuals. A typical herd might be 6 ewes, 6 lambs, and 2 yearlings. The rams group together and run independently of the others, except for the rutting season in the fall when they rejoin the rest.

The sheep are amply capable of spending winters at high altitude but the ewes and lambs generally work lower when deep snow covers their food. Bighorn eat numerous alpine plants including sedges, shorthair grass, buttercups, wild buckwheat, and mountain sorrel. A favorite is a wooly, yellow-flowered plant named *Hulsea algida* that belongs to the sunflower family and grows in decomposed granite at altitudes of 11,000 to 14,000 feet. The sheep not only eat the leaves and stems but dig up the carrot-like roots with their hooves.[8] Bighorn rest in simple depressions pawed in the ground. The oval bed is roughly the shape of the sheep's body and is merely a shallow hollow scraped bare of loose rock by a few quick motions of a forefoot. The sheep often rest during the day to chew their cuds and once bedded down are almost impossible to see.

Early accounts of California tell of many bands of wild sheep in the Sierra Nevada but the twin scourges of hunters and diseases introduced from Europe with the importation of domestic sheep caused the death of thousands. Still worse in the long run was the competition for food between the bighorn and domestic sheep and cattle. The summer and winter pastures of the bighorn were stripped bare by overzealous herders. "Weakened by disease and unable to find enough to eat, the thinning bands of bighorn wandered over their denuded range," wrote one authority. "When the winter storms came, more bighorn died of hunger,

disease, and exhaustion than had been shot during the summer by the meat and trophy hunters."[9]

By 1912, two observers reported the bighorn extinct.[10] Fortunately these writers were wrong. Though decimated, the surviving sheep still existed in the higher and more remote areas away from man and the problems he caused. (It has been against the law to hunt bighorn in California since 1883 but poaching by deer hunters has been recorded as recently as 1935 and again in 1954.[11] By 1900, bighorn had disappeared from Yosemite entirely. In 1931, State Game Warden E. H. Ober estimated that about 200 sheep existed south of Mammoth Pass but the future of the species seemed doubtful and many people thought the bighorn would soon join the passenger pigeon in oblivion.

In 1948, Fred Jones, a biologist working on an advanced degree at the University of California, undertook a major study of Sierra bighorn. He made a careful search of everything that had been written and interviewed dozens of people from Mammoth Lakes to Tehachapi regarding sheep sightings. After a year of solo climbing and observations in the bighorn territory—certainly an heroic and commendable feat—Jones summarized both his records and those of others, eliminating possible duplications, to arrive at a population figure of 390 bighorn. According to Jones there were five herds: Convict Creek herd, Birch Mt. herd, Mt. Baxter herd, Mt. Williamson herd, and Mt. Langley herd. Jones observed sheep and abundant tracks, bedding sites, and droppings in three of the five locations. He confirmed the Birch Mountain herd by tracks only ("six ewes and lambs at an elevation of 13,200 feet on the east side of The Thumb"). The Convict Creek herd was estimated by reliable reports of others. Jones thought the low point of sheep population had been passed "and that with proper protection and management the Sierra bighorn can be restored, if not to former numbers, at least to a safe and permanent population."[12]

Jones pointed out that overgrazing by deer and domestic livestock on the eastern slope of the Sierra has caused the native grass—herb climax growth to be widely replaced by shrubs unpalatable to bighorn. Since World War II, livestock grazing has been reduced to some extent which has allowed partial recovery of the bighorn winter range, and this may account for their increase. During severe winters however, the bighorn are forced even lower, into areas where heavy over-grazing has occurred and where large deer populations tend to take the winter feed. Competition from deer and the lack of adequate browse may be limiting factors in bighorn population growth.[13]

Scabies, the serious disease formerly caught from domestic sheep, is presumably gone, since all domestic sheep are now periodically dipped.

When I set about taking the photographs for this book I hoped to get good pictures of bighorn sheep and during the years that I have worked on this project I have always had a camera ready. Though I looked long and often, I had no luck. In 1962 while camped near Center Peak I talked with two Boy Scouts who had seen two ewes and a ram on University Peak the day before. Their account and descriptions made sense and there was no doubt that they had made actual sightings. My climbing, however, merely resulted in the finding of several recent bedding sites on the east side of Center Peak just above the abandoned trail to Junction Pass. In 1963 I spent a week in the same area during August. One day while climbing University Peak from the University Pass side I came around a great outcropping of rocks and—lo and behold!—there stood a small sandy-colored ewe bighorn about 100 feet away. I had my Nikon on my shoulder with a 200 mm. lens all focused and set and I had rehearsed what I would do many times. But from surprise or exhaustion of the climb (I was at 13,000 feet, after a morning of scrambling up some evil looking places) or possibly the altitude, I hesitated for a second and just looked at the bighorn. She looked back, with her head cocked to her left—and turned and disappeared among rocks that were the identical color of her coat. My first interview with a bighorn had ended. I was astonished and amazed and I had—and have —no photograph.

I must content myself with the following description of 14 bighorn seen by Russell Keene on the west slope of Black Mountain, just east of Rae Lakes, in Kings Canyon National Park in 1940.

". . . [while I was scaling Black Mountain] my attention was attracted by the sound of falling rocks some three hundred yards from me across a ravine. At one brief glance I saw . . . a band of fourteen Sierra Bighorn sheep. They were at an elevation of approximately 12,500 feet, and as near as I could judge there were at least three rams, while three or four of the others appeared to be quite small, as if they might have been spring lambs. For years I had been looking forward to . . . just one glimpse of these magnificent creatures in action in their native haunts among the crags and sky pastures of the great snow peaks; and then . . . there they were before my astonished eyes, bounding from rock to rock, from ledge to ledge, and up steep chimneys where it seemed utterly impossible for living creatures to travel.

". . . in traversing comparatively gentle slopes, the animals ran in single file, but while negotiating cliffs and precipitous slopes they would invariably spread out, each animal selecting its own path to avoid falling rocks dislodged by its companions. Twice they were compelled to cross precipitous chutes or slides tilted at the dizzy angle of something like sixty degrees, imprisoned between vertical rock walls; the bottoms of these chutes were covered with a loose decomposed granite devoid of any kind of footing. The Bighorns fully realizing the lack of footing here would leap down off the walls and race across the chutes at great speed, being carried across by sheer momentum amid a shower of flying talus. Only one . . . crossed at a time, while the others stood by . . . and the ones that crossed over waited until all the others had joined them before proceeding up the rocks."[14]

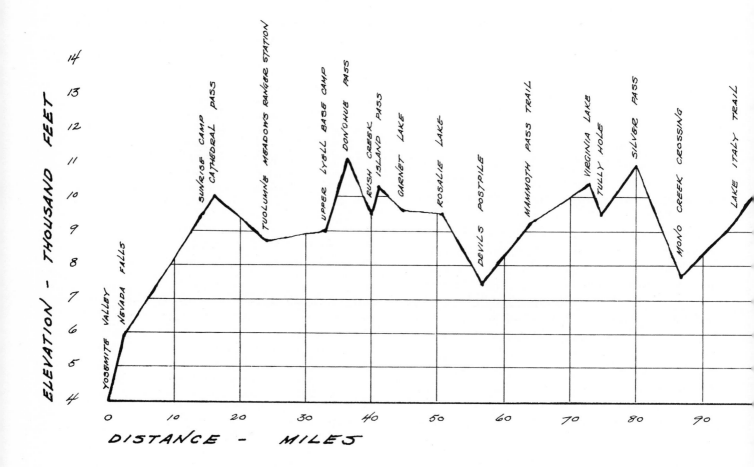

ELEVATION - THOUSAND FEET

14
13
12
11
10
9
8
7
6
5
4

YOSEMITE VALLEY
NEVADA FALLS
SUNRISE CAMP
CATHEDRAL PASS
TUOLUMNE MEADOWS RANGER STATION
UPPER LYELL BASE CAMP
DONOHUE PASS
RUSH CREEK
ISLAND PASS
GARNET LAKE
ROSALIE LAKE
DEVILS POSTPILE
MAMMOTH PASS TRAIL
VIRGINIA LAKE
TULLY HOLE
SILVER PASS
MONO CREEK CROSSING
LAKE ITALY TRAIL

0   10   20   30   40   50   60   70   80   90

DISTANCE - MILES

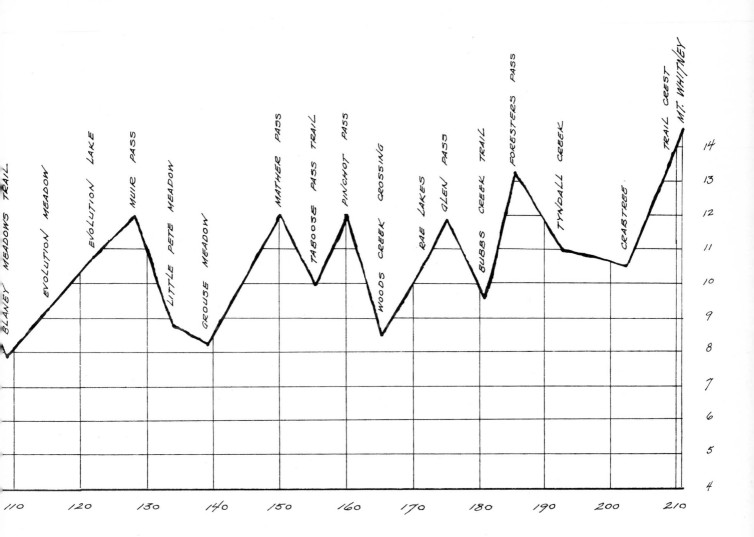

Elevation Graph . . . The John Muir Trail

Elevation Graph . . . The John Muir Trail

Approaching Forester Pass

Dawn along the trail near Center Basin. Here we have a backdrop of Center Peak with its great western slope still in shadow. Behind the lodgepole pine to the right we can see the triangular face of Junction Peak. (Right.) Un-named spur of the Kings-Kern Divide northeast of Forester Pass. How jagged and precipitous are these peaks. And so many!

The Rocky Trail

Just before the final climb to Forester Pass the trail touches a large, rock-bound lake tucked away at the head of a glacial cirque. The lake is un-named and marked on the map only by its elevation, 12,248. A few hundred yards below the lake the trail crosses a moraine, a typical jumbled up composite of earth and large and small stones all piled helter-skelter. In the photograph the trail looks narrow and frightfully dangerous but in reality the track is wide enough for a pack train. The rocks above are relatively well settled. Sometimes moraines such as these cover ice. A few years ago Dana Abell discovered one such mud-covered glacial fragment less than a mile from Forester Pass.

We see two Boy Scouts carefully picking their way along the trail. The walking here is easy, the main problem being shortness of breath caused by the two-mile-high-plus altitude. Surprisingly, downhill hiking is much harder on the body and feet than going uphill. In going down an uneven pathway that frequently turns, you are constantly braking and stopping and starting which results in continual jolts on your body. During each jerk, the whole force of your body's weight (plus the weight of your backpack if you are carrying one) is concentrated on your feet which often respond with a few aches and sometimes blisters. Hiking uphill, on the other hand, is a different business in which your muscles are coordinated and work smoothly with one another to force your weight upward without such fatiguing sudden up and down motions.

THE ROCKY TRAIL

37

GLEN PASS TO MT. WHITNEY
Girl Packer

Margery Twining was 18 years old the summer these photographs were taken. "It was a wonderful life," she says. 'We got up when the dawn was only an inky blue and went out after the animals, tracking them across the frosty meadows. I got to know all the mules—Kate, Judy, Sis, Joan, Cricket —and they became great friends. The pack stock knew their jobs so well that they rebelled when I did something wrong and patiently resisted until I learned the right way to tie on a pack or to take them across snow. I thought I had found out all about horses at our home ranch in Ukiah but out in the wilderness you have to do everything your-self—from pulling off twisted horseshoes to keeping the animals happy in the morning with a few handfulls from a sack of barley we carried.

"I didn't get paid much in dollars that summer but money really didn't matter somehow. It was the experience of the outdoors that counted. How I remember it all—the smoky fires, the icy mornings, the mule that disappeared, the jokes at suppertime, the argument with the cook about the broken eggs, the hot sun at noon . . . When I went back to college that fall I really missed it. How I would like to go back!"

GLEN PASS TO MT. WHITNEY

GIRL PACKER

GIRL PACKER

Un-named Lake

HEADWATERS OF THE KERN RIVER

From a distance the mountains sometimes seem hard and barren—wastelands of dull rocks with frightening extremes of climate, uninviting and inhospitable. But when you walk closer the distant wrinkles soften and open into green canyons slashed by silvery streams; far-away glints become flashing lakes of blue. Fingers of forest reach up toward the ridges and the delicious shade of the pines brings coolness on a summer's noon. A meadow from ten miles is a dot; from five miles a circle of green; from one mile an oasis; from the spot a dream.

Something reddish-brown blurs the edge of your vision and you turn to watch a furry marmot climb on top of a rock and sit regarding you. In the lee of a boulder at your feet you suddenly notice a red bouquet of Indian paintbrush and the nodding purple flowers on a clump of alpine shoot-

ing stars. You stop to sniff the pungent herbage of the pennyroyal plant. Somewhere nearby a stream tumbles and splashes. Like anything alien, the foreigness begins to vanish with familiarity.

What's down by the tributary stream and around the bend? Let's go and see . . . Perhaps no one has ever walked this way before. We stop a moment. Wait! What are those chips of shiny black rock? Obsidian? There seems to be a trail of the black rock slivers leading toward the lake. Let's follow them. Look! The rock has pounding holes for acorns. We have found an ancient Indian stopping place, a site where Indian women prepared acorn meal while the men chipped heads for arrows and spears. The fragments of rock we followed were flakes from the chipping . . . How unwild the wilderness can suddenly be!

UN-NAMED LAKE

"There is nothing more fascinating than going 'over the top' at a pass—the thrill, the excitement, the mystery of what is beyond! You plod up and up, ever watching your step; over rough rocks, rolling and sliding; over loose, steep shale and sand. You are out of breath; you are weary; the blazing sun beats down upon you; you may say, 'What's the use?'—when all at once you reach the top and get that grand expansive view and look over into a promised land, on to weird snow-fields, to silvery, flashing streams, down into azure lakes, up to ragged peaks, into the purest of pure air and the bluest of blue skies. It is the call of the high country; the call of the Main Crest; the call toward heaven! It is irresistible."

. . . J. S. HUTCHINSON
writing of mountain travel
[Sierra Club *Bulletin*, 1923, p. 361]

203

38

GLEN PASS TO MT. WHITNEY
The Foxtail Pines of Tyndall Bench

In 1850, a group of Edinburgh Scotsmen formed a botanical association called the Oregon Committee of Scotland. One of their first acts was to raise money to send a young gardener named John Jeffrey to the wilds of America to collect new species of trees. Jeffrey first went to Hudson's Bay and gradually worked his way west. By diligence and hard work he discovered five new conifers and delighted his patrons with specimens of the new cones and seeds and leaves that he dispatched home by clipper ship. By the spring of 1851 the capable Jeffrey was on the Pacific Coast near Mt. Baker in what later became the State of Washington, continuing his lonely task far ahead of civilization. In 1852 he entered California and in its northern mountains found the foxtail pine which he named *Pinus balfouriana* in honor of John Balfour, professor of botany at the University of Edinburgh. The following year Jeffrey disappeared in San Francisco and regrettably was never heard of again.[1]

The pine that Jeffrey discovered occurs in California in the north Coast Range and in the Sierra Nevada south of Woods Creek. Beginning at Rae Lakes and going south you find almost pure stands at high altitudes—up to 12,000 feet—on typically barren, rocky, windswept sites. "Just some old dying trees," you might say after a quick look. But if you inspect a grove of foxtail pines carefully you will find them surprisingly healthy and thriving; their appearance is ragged because of their harsh environment.

The leaves of this evergreen occur in a fat, closely-clustered bundle of five which measures ¾ to 1 inch long. The bundle is a medium apple-green outside and whitish inside. Viewed from the end the five individual needles of a single cluster fit together to make a perfect circle, each needle taking one-fifth of 360°. The thick, bushy foliage surrounds the end of each branch for 10 to 20 inches and readily suggests the common name of the tree.

The cones are slender and egg-shaped, 2½ inches long and 1¾ to 2 inches thick. They mature and open during August of every other year when they are a bright purple dotted with reddish-brown scales. Sometimes sap runs on the cones and turns the purples and reddish-browns into spangles of reflecting rainbows, decorating the tree with glittering cones that look like Christmas tree ornaments. The seeds fall from the cones in September, followed several months later by the dried cones.

During September, 1962, I camped near Tyndall Creek, a quarter of a mile east of the John Muir Trail immediately below and northwest of Tawny Point, 12,332 feet, a southwest spur of Mt. Tyndall. The camp was near several tiny lakes on a smooth bench at 11,120 feet altitude. Across from me on the slope running down from Tawny Point stood a grove of foxtail pines, a quarter of a mile long and perhaps 150 yards deep. I wondered how any trees could survive in such an environment, for the site seemed nothing but a mass of rocks and stood in a position exposed to tremendous winds that presumably blew up and down the canyon most of the year. I thought of snow and rock avalanches hurtling down to wreck the trees. I went to investigate.

The foxtail grove needed water of course but only a certain amount, and spring flooding from the small lake below the trees prevented growth around its shores. Fifty feet higher however, the land was drier and well-drained but still moist—perfect for the foxtail. The southeast slope got plenty of afternoon sun but not enough to dry out the rocky grove which surprisingly had some black soil underneath the boulders.

I counted 47 mature trees (including a few dead snags) in the Tyndall Bench grove. They were astonishingly vigorous, tall and straight with bright-green leaves, and bark colored a strong cinnamon-brown. The trees ran in age from young adults (two feet in circumference) to ancient giants (one measured 18.5 feet around). The circumferences of the 47 conifers averaged 7 feet 10 inches, or 2.5 feet in diameter, not bad for trees growing above 11,000 feet. The grove was pure foxtail pine with the exception of one lodgepole 4 feet tall. The trunk of the largest tree was partially hollowed out and birds had nested (or a marmot had hibernated) in the depression.

The shapes of the trees seemed well-suited to their location. The stocky branches were thick and strong with relatively little area to catch the wind; indeed I thought that if an imaginary narrow paper cylinder could be slipped down over each tree it would scarcely touch the branches so restricted was their reach. The silhouette of the foxtail is like no other tree. It is short and thickset, and shows heavy clusters of brush-like leaves on a few low branches rather than the leisurely, less compact leafing of conifers that grow at lower altitudes.

Typically half the bark was gone from each tree and the exposed wood had long wavy vertical cracks. Often the entire top one-third was stripped of bark and foliage and reflected a hard metallic yellow glare where wind-driven grit had sand-blasted the wood. The trees seemed to die from the top down and it was usual to see a bleached snag sticking up from a mass of intense green foliage which always occurred close enough to the ground so that even on a large tree you could reach up and touch fresh leaves. The younger trees seemed to have the most foliage; perhaps this was because the leaves of the newer trees were evenly distributed on branches up and down the trunk while on the older trees they were concentrated on a few low branches. I expected massive bark on the foxtail, but it was thin and smooth and chalky-brown on young trees and scarcely heavy (1 to 1½ inches thick) on older trees where it was lightly furrowed into squarish plates. Exposed roots had heavier bark which was strongly broken into distinct sections. Wherever there had been an injury to the bark or a branch, sap flowed freely.

I counted 115 seedlings under three feet high scattered among the trees. The new growth was concentrated somewhat at either end of the grove rather than the center, perhaps to get away from the shade of the older trees but still closely tied to the grove by the water table (too wet below; too dry above). One seedling 5 inches high had a root 6½ inches long.

Some of the trees had a slight counterclockwise twist which was most evident on old snags that had fallen. There were burned fragments all through the grove—evidence that lightning had struck many times—and a lot of the standing trees had charred parts. The clues may be stronger than the facts however, for the charred wood seems extremely resistant to decay and may easily lie around for hundreds of years. The litter on the ground was mostly cones, dry needles, and tiny twigs rather than branches because the foxtail doesn't have many limbs. Instead of branches falling from time to time after they die, the short powerful limbs stay on the trunk until the entire tree finally comes down, which is infrequent because the roots tend to grow around large rocks that anchor the tree, and hold it even after it dies. Marmots often live among the complicated root structure of old trees.

The slope behind the grove appeared steep and an ideal place for avalanches, but I believe it looks worse than it is. The rocks were well settled and though no doubt an occasional boulder rumbles through the grove, I could discover no direct avalanche damage.

The foxtail pine is closely related to the bristlecone pine *(Pinus aristata)* found in the White Mountains, the next range to the east. The bristlecone grows to incredible ages—many 2,000 and 3,000-year-old specimens are known—but the foxtail seems a younger relation and not given to the colossal multiple trunks of the bristlecone.

How life flourished in the small grove on Tyndall Bench! The trees held clusters of new cones and the rich browns of the bark glowed golden in the warm sun. Bees hummed everywhere. Sparrows flitted about. Chipmunks dashed from rock to rock, their nervous tails held high. A round-eared cony squeaked out a greeting while perched on a clump of grass. I reached up to feel the bushy needles on a foxtail branch and got instead a palmful of sticky sap. As I sat down to wipe the viscous resin from my hand I leaned back and thought how healthy and vigorous it all seemed. What vitality was in the grove! What I had thought were "just some old dying trees" were as full of life as a youngster in the morning.

I returned to my little camp with a new respect for the plant world and humble realization that life in any form has incredible strength and amazing adaptability to its environment

39

GLEN PASS TO MT. WHITNEY
The Highest Peak

Mt. Whitney, the southern terminus of the John Muir Trail, is the highest peak in the United States, except for those in Alaska, and pokes up to a cloud-scraping 14,496 feet. In spite of its height however, the mountain is not prominent at all, being merely a high tooth roughly in the middle of a serrated crest that runs along at 14,000 feet for 17 miles between Shepherd Pass on the north and Cottonwood Pass to the south.[1] The mountain itself is hard to see from a distance. In fact when people look for Mt. Whitney from the little town of Lone Pine, far below in Owens Valley to the east, someone has to point the mountain out to them from amidst a mass of hills, ridges, spurs, and peaks that make up the precipitous great eastern wall of the Sierra Nevada that rises two miles above the valley.

The mountain was named in 1864 by the four chief assistants of the State Geological Survey Party to honor their leader, Josiah D. Whitney, an eminent geologist of the day. Clarence King, a member of the survey group, repeatedly tried to climb the mountain but failed through bad luck, poor weather, and ill-chosen routes. It was first climbed in 1873 by three men of Inyo County, John Lucas, Charles Begole, and Albert H. Johnson who made their ascent from Crabtree Meadow to the southwest, the same route the John Muir Trail now follows.[2]

Since the mountain was so high, astronomers decided it would be ideal for observations. In 1881 a trail up the west side was roughed over the worst places for the supply animals of Professor Samuel P. Langley, later well known for his aviation experiments, and a group of scientists who wanted to measure heat from the sun. The trail was gradually improved as others trod to the summit, some via Crabtree Meadow while others went by way of Lone Pine Canyon directly from Owens Valley.

In 1903, a prominent meteorologist recommended that a weather observatory be built on the summit. The people of Lone Pine, anxious for the scientific station, undertook to improve the trail. When the work was finished the following year, there was a suitable celebration on top. "We had a large fire at night," wrote the leader, "and fireworks which were plainly seen [by those] at Lone Pine, who responded with a large fire and fireworks." Unfortunately nothing came of the weather station suggestion.[3]

In August of 1908, Dr. C. G. Abbot of the Smithsonian Institution met on the summit with the director of Lick Observatory, Dr. W. W. Campbell, to scout the possibilities of observing heavenly bodies. Abbot wanted to study solar radiation. Campbell was keen to measure the water pressure on Mars. The chief obstacle up to that time had been the conflict with water vapor in the atmosphere of the earth; from high on Whitney it was hoped that this troublesome interference would be eliminated.

After spending a freezing, windy night on the summit the two men decided that a strong shelter would be needed. The directors of the Smithsonian Institution liked the idea and appropriated money for a summit house to be built of masonry, glass, and steel and to be open to researchers of all branches of science. To get the materials to the summit the trail had to be rebuilt. It had not been very good in the first place and the efforts of five years before had largely tumbled down from lack of regular maintenance. In April, 1909, the people of Lone Pine held a ball to raise funds. The festivity was a grand success and trail work was started as soon as the snows had melted. The first mules reached the summit on July 28, and the shelter, under the energetic command of G. F. Marsh, was finished in exactly one month.

eft) Pinnacles along the trail just south of the summit of Whitney

This excellent trail leads from Guitar Lake to the summit of Whitney. *(Top, at right)*. Whitney from the Bighorn Plateau. This view to the east southeast shows the broad curving back of the great peak. The foreground trees are mostly foxtail pines. *(Bottom, at right)*. Whitney from the east near Crabtree Ranger Station. From an elevation here of 10,600 feet we are too low to see more than a mass of low spires and sharp vertical ridges on the back of the mountain. The soil is quite sandy along Whitney Creek in the foreground and we see a good growth of young and old lodgepole pines.

Looking to the south from near the summit of Whitney your eye travels along this series of notches and teeth on the broad ascending back of the peak. The trail here works up to the summit of Whitney from the south and we can just make out the faint line of the pathway on the roughly 40° slope. As the trail passes each of the east-facing notches you hold your breath and peer down thousands of feet into the heads of ancient glacial cirques and the distant desert scenery of Owens Valley and the dry lands beyond. The picture at right looks south from near the junction to Trail Crest.

On Friday about noon [wrote Dr. Abbot on August 27], three of us being seated about the stove, one of the workmen tried to show us how convenient a Smith & Wesson hammerless revolver is for shooting from the pocket. He forgot it was loaded, and it went off bang! and struck the stove pipe in the corner of the room. Fortunately nobody was hurt and the stove pipe was too thick to penetrate so that the bullet fell at his feet. This celebrated the completion of the house.[4]

The scientists were plagued by severe and continuing lightning storms and bad weather but they persevered.

"On the second trip [in 1909] the object was to test the truth of Professor Lowell's statement that Mars was inhabited," wrote Professor Alexander McAdie. "It was a favorable period and the astronomers made spectrograms from which the constitution of the atmosphere of Mars was to be determined. . . . The season was a rainy one. Instead of being the 'land of little rain,' we had some five out of seven rainy days. We had thunderstorms *below* us. On one occasion the hairs on the burros stood out straight and at the same time a brass button on my cap over my left temple gave little sparks. . . . I think if the storm had been a trifle more intense there would have been four or five dead astronomers on the summit."[5]

The wet weather ruined the measurements of water vapor on Mars and the experiments were stopped. Dr. Abbot's observations of solar radiation were successful however, and he continued his work the following year. It was tricky business packing delicate and cumbersome equipment on the trails that then existed. "The good fortune which had attended the 1909 expedition failed for a moment in 1910, and one mule, carrying the silver-disc pyrheliometer and other loading, rolled off among the rocks and was killed," noted Dr. Abbot. "The pyrheliometer fortunately received no injury."[6]

THE HIGHEST PEAK

In 1913 the Swedish physicist Anders Angström and a party of U. S. scientists used the observatory and shelter to investigate radiation of the atmosphere. The same year two meteorologists studied the upper air of the earth by using small weather balloons which were filled with gas and allowed to rise on long wires wound on hand reels. The highest balloon ascension was 3,082 feet or 17,578 feet above sea level, then a record height.

Since 1913 the summit house has not been maintained and has become a disgraceful dump for litter and trash from climbers.

The John Muir Trail zigzags up the west side of Whitney from Crabtree Meadow to Trail Crest, the junction with the east side Whitney Trail, where it swings northward to the summit. The present trail is excellent—wide and well-graded—and is in no way dangerous, only fatiguing and best taken slowly. Each year about 2,000 people climb Whitney between June and October. Most start out from Whitney Portal, the end of the road from Lone Pine, and follow the very steep and strenuous trail which has a rise of over 6,000 feet in 14 miles.

An amazing assortment of people make it to the top. Some are right out of the funny papers. History records that one man walked barefoot, another pushed a wheelbarrow, and someone tried to ride a bicycle. Not long ago three youths attempted to push a motorcycle to the summit (unsuccessful). Some climbers bundle up in heavy coats, some wear bathing suits, and some wear nothing at all (several years ago a group of nudists signed the summit register). One man went to the top done up in a fashionable business suit with a fedora and bow tie and carried his blankets and food in a suitcase.[7]

But though the bizarre and eccentric make the newspapers and illustrated magazines, most climbers are ordinary souls bent on going up the great mountain for the experience and wonderful views.

At the far left is the conventional view of Whitney from the trail. The summit itself is at the left on top of the almost horizontal plateau. If you strain a little you can just make out the shelter on top.

The top of Whitney is surprising. Instead of a steep cone or a ragged fist of cracked rock it has a large flat summit several acres in size that slopes first gently then increasingly steeply toward the west. The broad, slowly curving back of Whitney, a remnant of an ancient Sierra, was once a hill, probably about 2,000 feet high, that was gradually uplifted and tilted along with the massive block of the Sierra as the range was uplifted during millions of years. In time rivers furrowed deeply into the mountains and channeled out large valleys and canyons. During the Ice Age the top of Whitney remained serenely above the ice, though glaciers were all around, cutting especially deeply on the northern and eastern slopes where they were shaded from the erosive rays of the hot sun. The resulting glacial cirques worked back farther and farther toward the heart of the mountain and if the Ice Age hadn't ended would in time have chewed away the present summit by undercutting its eastern and northern faces. On the way to the top you pass a series of notches on the right from which you can look directly down thousands of feet into the heads of these ancient glacial cirques and see where the glacial ice—by plucking and frost action —worked back into the mountain.

When you look from the summit on a clear day the colors are wonderful: the inky blacks of distant lakes; the turquoise of nearer ones neatly rimmed with circles of white ice. The deep rust red of the Kaweah peaks to the west. The fine-grained whitish granite at your feet. The incredible blackness of the three-mile-high sky at the zenith shading away to lighter and lighter blues as your eyes level with the horizon. The purplish light over Owens Valley as the atmosphere—back-lighted by the sun as you rest after your morning climb—turns violet. Far below are stabbing accents of green, tiny meadows where new earth has collected and plants burst forth.

When you look from the summit of Whitney the geometry of the world below seems like a world in a dream! Laid out before your eyes are massive granite bosses, valleys and canyons, moraines, slopes of talus and scree, frost-fractured rock, pinnacles, fingers of granite, avalanche slopes, and peaks cascading away to infinity toward the eastern deserts—so much that you need an afternoon and a map to figure it all out. But even more, such an afternoon gives you a chance to figure yourself out—and to see how you fit—or don't fit— in the vast world we live in.

40

PATHWAY IN THE SKY
The Future

What is wilderness when it becomes burdened with rules? Is it wilderness any longer? One reason people go to wild places is to get away from restrictions. In the old days you could hunt and fish and camp and graze your animals when and where you pleased. If you wanted boughs for a bed you could cut them without reproach. You drank freely from streams because water contamination was unknown. You didn't need a fishing license or a deer tag, and you could carry a gun and take your dog anywhere. The tradition of the wilderness was freedom from rules because your actions interferred with no one else.

But our country no longer has large unpopulated places. Those that are left are mere islands of park and forest protected by state and federal governments. Just about all private land has been hacked clear of natural beauty by people intent on the profit from the land. (Have you ever seen a private park?) Each year the number of people in the United States increases, with California, the most populous state, growing by 1,600 *people a day*.[1] Not only are there more people but each works fewer hours to support himself. Experts tell us that the Age of Leisure is upon us.

How many people travel on the John Muir Trail? How much use does the 6,000 square miles of the High Sierra get? Total back country travel in Sequoia and Kings Canyon National Parks totaled 65,000 camper days in 1953. By 1960 the figure rose to 127,000 camper days or about double. Burro use increased from 3,500 burro days to 5,000 burro days during the same period while horse and mule use declined slightly.[2]

Registers to tabulate travel have long been put at various passes and park entrance points. You would think that such registers would give reliable travel figures, but observations by park rangers

have shown that only about 50 per cent of passersby sign. Mounted parties often don't stop and the absence of a pencil (!) is a factor. Registrations plus careful estimates of travel in Sequoia-Kings Canyon at four places on the John Muir Trail follow.[3]

	1953	1957
Goddard Canyon	200	316
McClure Meadow	600	866
Little Pete Meadow	425	763
Crabtree Meadow	268	510

In 1962, analysis of campfire permits in Sequoia-Kings Canyon showed that 1,936 backpackers and 1,023 people traveling with stock used the southern third of the John Muir Trail during the summer. The campfire permit study, which appears to be more accurate than trail registers, noted that only 24 per cent of back country travel was with stock, a high percentage of which (43%) was by burro or walking mule parties. The country between Muir and Mather Passes was crossed by 486 backpackers and 193 people with animals in 1962.[4]

Further north in Sierra National Forest the district ranger estimated in 1963 that "2,000 people get into Bear Creek each summer, about 1,800 go up Mono Creek, and 1,200 travel into the Quail Meadow-Silver Pass area. I estimate that 3,000 to 3,500 travel from Florence Lake up the South Fork of the San Joaquin toward Evolution. In all I figure that about 12,000 people visit the High Sierra Wilderness Area every summer."[5]

Nearer Yosemite, an Inyo National Forest recreational aide at Shadow Lake tabulated 9,040 man-days use in 1962. The following year the figure rose to 12,000 man-days, and in 1964 the number was 13,400. Based on fire permits, officials in Yosemite estimated that 3,600 people traveled on the John Muir Trail in 1964. "On the basis of fire permits, general observation, and tent camp counts it is estimated that more than 50,000 persons spent approximately 150,000 use days in the back country of Yosemite," wrote David de L. Condon, acting superintendent of Yosemite, in February, 1965.

We tend to blame the people in charge of anything with responsibility for all problems inherent in management when often we cause the very problem we cry about loudest. I gnash my teeth when I think of more rules in the John Muir Trail country but I agree with one back country study which said the trouble is not "bureaucracy" but "born too late."[6] Or as Ranger Arn Snyder has said, ". . . when we speak loosely of an 'untouched' wilderness we must actually be reconciled and receptive to an area managed in a degree relative to the number of people who enter it."[7]

What will the beautiful John Muir Trail country be like in ten years? One hundred years? Will it have been cut and trampled and eroded to death? Or will modest controls keep it fresh and beautiful as it is now so that a visit to a Sierra meadow in the fullness of its summer perfection will be a pleasure and a thrill? Will the John Muir Trail country have been fragmented and ruined by roads? It seems to me that arguments for the proposed road across the Sierra at Mammoth Pass and elsewhere have little validity. At best such roads would be open four months of the year. If the proponents of roads would take the blinders of niggling commercial gain from their eyes, perhaps they would see *what the area means to the whole American people, now and in the future.* Every new road leads to one less wilderness area. We have plenty of roads; we have few wilderness areas. And those left belong to a population that is growing mightily.

The people of the United States must keep a few wild places. Far too much of our country has been cut and carved and bulldozed to death. Can't we hold on to a few samples of wilderness that are capable of giving the viewer a delicious sense of the beauty, order, and perfection of untouched nature? It's easy to take it away. But once it's gone it can never be put back. Let's hold just a little of our country aside and keep it as it was in the beginning. Let's treat it gently and with respect. It's our native land.

Star Streaks

Notes and References

SECTIONS 1-6

[1]Based on tabulation from *A Climber's Guide to the High Sierra*, San Francisco, Sierra Club, 1954.

[2]Francis P. Farquhar, *Exploration of the Sierra Nevada*, Calif. Historical Society, San Francisco, 1925, pp. 4-5; also Harrison Clifford Dale, *Ashley-Smith Explorations and the Discovery of a Central Route to the Pacific 1822-1829*, Cleveland, Arthur H. Clark Company, 1918, p. 183.

[3]Farquhar, op. cit., pp. 6-7; also John W. Caughey, *California*, 2nd ed. N. Y., Prentice-Hall [1953], pp. 197-199; quote from Zenas Leonard, *Narrative of the Adventures of Zenas Leonard*, Chicago, R. R. Donnelley, 1934, p. 136.

[4]Farquhar, op. cit., p. 8.

[5]Farquhar, ibid., pp. 8-10.

[6]Dr. Lafayette Houghton Bunnell, *Discovery of the Yosemite and the Indian War of 1851*, Chicago, Fleming H. Revell [1880], p. 70.

[7]W. A. Chalfant, *Story of Inyo*, 1933, p. 124.

[8]J. D. Whitney, *Geological Survey of California*, State of Calif., 1865, Vol. I, pp. 364-395.

[9]William H. Brewer, *Up and Down California in 1860-1864*, Berkeley, Univ. of Calif. Press, 1949, pp. 515-516.

[10]Clarence King, *Mountaineering in the Sierra Nevada*, N. Y., Norton [1935], pp. 69-70.

[11]Brewer, op. cit.

[12]Brewer, ibid., pp. 529-534; also see E. C. Winchell, "Kings River Cañon in 1868," *Sierra Club Bulletin*, XII, 1924, pp. 237-249.

[13]For the earliest trips into Tehipite Valley and the Middle Fork of the Kings and mention of Frank Dusy, "Little Pete" Giraud, and Pete Rambaud, see Francis P. Farquhar, "Early History of the Kings River Sierra," *Sierra Club Bulletin*, XXVI, Feb. 1941, pp. 38-39.

[14]Caughey, op. cit., p. 107.

[15]Marion Lee Menzel, *Historical Geography of the Sheep Industry in California in the Nineteenth Century*, University of Calif. Thesis, Oct. 1944. An excellent, well researched historical survey of domestic sheep in California.

[16]John Hayes, "Sheep-Farming in California," *The Overland Monthly*, Vol. 8, June 1872, p. 490.

[17]Menzel, op. cit.

[18]Robert Laxalt, *Sweet Promised Land*, N. Y., Harper & Bros. [1957]. Also Menzel p. 58. Laxalt's excellent book gives a sympathetic picture of the sheepherder who has been almost completely scorned in the literature of the West.

[19]Wilson Flint, "Textile Fibres of the Pacific States," *Transactions*, Calif. State Agricultural Society, 1864-65, p. 284, as quoted in Menzel, op. cit., p. 31.

[20]Memorandum from G. M. Spurlock, UC, Davis.

[21]The early herders were amazingly industrious. Prior to 1879 they had run sheep even in the Enchanted Gorge and Disappearing Creek area south of Mt. Goddard, one of the roughest regions in the whole range, seldom visited since. See *Sierra Club Bulletin*, XII, 1924, p. 20 for statement by Lil A. Winchell. Also Francis P. Farquhar, *Sierra Club Bulletin*, XXVI, 1941, pp. 38-39.

[22]Report of the California State Board of Agriculture for the year 1911, State of Calif., 1912, p. 82.

[23]John Muir, *My First Summer in the Sierra*, N. Y., Houghton Mifflin [1916], p. 195, p. 204; "Hoofed Locusts," quotation from *Son of the Wilderness: The Life of John Muir*, by Linnie Marsh Wolfe, N. Y., Alfred A. Knopf, 1951, p. 245. By far the best work on Muir.

[24]*Sierra Club Bulletin*, II, Jan. 1899, pp. 292-293.

[25]King, op. cit., p. 295.

[26]Marsden Manson, "Denudation of Vegetation," *Sierra Club Bulletin*, II, June 1899, p. 299.

[27]Arthur W. Sampson and Leon H. Weyl, *Range Preservation and its Relation to Erosion Control on Western Grazing Lands* (Washington, 1918), p. 2, as quoted in Menzel, op. cit., p. 72.

[28]Will C. Barnes, *Western Grazing Grounds and Forest Ranges* (Chicago, 1913), p. 217, as quoted in Menzel, op. cit., p. 69.

[29]A boundary adjustment in 1905 removed the Banner-Ritter area south of the park, an area in the west largely in private ownership, and added the Tuolumne watershed. Yosemite Valley, under control of the state since 1864, was given to the U. S. See Report of the Acting Superintendent Yosemite National Park 1892-1914, 1905 p. 5, 1906 p. 8.

[29a]A. E. Wood, "Report of the Acting Superintendent of the Yosemite National Park" 1892, p. 663.

[30]N. F. McClure, "Explorations Among the Cañons North of the Tuolumne River," *Sierra Club Bulletin*, I, Jan. 1895, pp. 168-170.

[31]*Sierra Club Bulletin*, I, Jan. 1896, p. 274.

[32]Mary Austin, *The Flock*, Cambridge, Houghton Mifflin, The Riverside Press, 1906, p. 192.

[33]Francis P. Farquhar, "Colonel Benson," *Sierra Club Bulletin*, XII, 1925, p. 176.

[33a]J. W. Zevely, "Report of the Acting Superintendent of the Yosemite National Park," 1898, p. 3.

[33b]Joseph E. Caine, "Report of the Acting Superintendent of the Yosemite National Park," 1898.

[34]Sporadic mining on a small scale has continued from time to time, mostly on the eastern slopes. A molybdenum claim was worked on upper Shadow Creek in the early

1950s and claims have been made on Bishop Creek and at Mammoth Lakes. The only significant present-day mining is for tungsten near Bishop.

[35]Account of Thomas Keough, *Sierra Club Bulletin*, X, 1918, pp. 341-342.

[36]William F. Badé, *Life and Letters of John Muir*, N. Y., Houghton Mifflin, 1923, v. 1, p. 154.

[37]Wolfe, op. cit., p. 105.

[38]John Muir, *My First Summer in the Sierra*, N. Y., Houghton Mifflin [1916], p. 101.

[39]Wolfe, op. cit., p. 163.

[40]Wolfe, ibid., 1.155.

[41]J. D. Whitney, *Yosemite Guide-Book*, Cambridge, Welch & Bigelow, 1869, p. 83-84.

[42]See foreword by John Buwalda in John Muir's *Studies in the Sierra*, San Francisco, Sierra Club [1960].

[43]John Muir, *Steep Trails*, N. Y., Houghton Mifflin [1918], p. 79.

[44]Wolfe, op. cit., p. 190.

[45]"The Clearest Way," University of California Explorer Radio Broadcast, Nov. 9, 1955, Script No. 3419, p. 3.

[46]Wolfe, op. cit., p. 244. Also see Robert Underwood Johnson, *Remembered Yesterdays*, Little, Brown, 1932, p. 278-9.

[47]Wolfe, ibid., p. 248.

[48]Wolfe, ibid., p. 144.

[49]Theodore S. Solomons, "The Beginnings of the John Muir Trail," *Sierra Club Bulletin*, XXV, 1940, p. 28.

[50]Theodore S. Solomons, "Among the Sources of the San Joaquin," *Sierra Club Bulletin*, I, Jan. 1894, p. 82.

[51]For an account of this trip see Theodore S. Solomons, "A Search for a High Mountain Route," *Sierra Club Bulletin*, I, May 1895, pp. 221-237.

[52]Theodore S. Solomons, "The Beginnings of the John Muir Trail," *Sierra Club Bulletin*, XXV, 1940, p. 33. Also see Appalachia VIII (1896-1898), pp. 41-57.

[53]Bolton Coit Brown, "Three Days with Mt. King," *Sierra Club Bulletin*, I, Jan. 1896, pp. 249-250.

[54]Bolton Coit Brown, "About the Headwaters of the King's River," *Sierra Club Bulletin*, I, May 1896, pp. 305-306.

[55]Bolton Coit Brown, "Another Paradise," *Sierra Club Bulletin*, III, May 1900, p. 139.

[56]J. S. Hutchinson, "Joseph Nisbet LeConte: Some Recollections," *Sierra Club Bulletin*, XXXV, 1950, p. 2.

[57]J. N. LeConte, "Among the Sources of the South Fork of King's River," *Sierra Club Bulletin*, IV, June 1903, p. 262. Evidentally LeConte forgot that Brown had climbed Arrow Peak in 1895 and Mt. Clarence King in 1896.

[58]J. N. LeConte, "The Evolution Group of Peaks," *Sierra Club Bulletin*, V, Jan. 1905, p. 236.

[59]Joseph N. LeConte, "The High Mountain Route between Yosemite and the King's River Cañon, *Sierra Club Bulletin*, VII, Jan. 1909, pp. 16-17.

[60]Walter L. Huber, "The John Muir Trail," *Sierra Club Bulletin*, XV, 1930, p. 37.

[61]Details from an interview with William E. Colby by Hal Roth dated Feb. 27-28, 1961. Transcript is in Bancroft Library, Univ. of Calif.

[62]Until its enlargement in 1926, Sequoia National Park was relatively small and located down the western slope. At the time of the early trail building, the southern area was all in Sequoia National Forest. Most of this area has since been included in Kings Canyon National Park, established in 1940.

[63]The exact route of the John Muir Trail is as follows: "Beginning at a point on the north floor of the Yosemite Valley and running from thence by the most practicable route northeasterly to a junction with the Tioga Road at a point near Tenaya Lake; thence northeasterly and easterly along and upon said Tioga Road to a point near the Soda Springs in the Tuolumne Meadows; thence in a general southeasterly direction up Lyell Cañon to the headwaters of said cañon, to and over Donohue Pass; thence in a general southeasterly direction across Rush Creek and Island Pass to Thousand Island Lake; thence easterly and southeasterly through Agnew Meadows, Pumice Flat, past Devils Post Pile, Reds Meadows, Fish Creek Valley, over Silver Pass, and thence by the most feasible route to the north fork of Mono Creek. Thence in a general southerly direction down the north fork of Mono Creek Valley, and Mono Creek Valley to Vermilion Valley; thence by the way of the present traveled trail southeasterly and southerly to Marie Lake and to and over Seldon Pass; thence continuing southerly and southeasterly along the valley of the south fork of the San Joaquin river to the mouth of Evolution Creek; thence continuing in a general southeasterly direction up Evolution Creek Valley, past Evolution Lake, Wanda Lake, over Muir Pass, down Le Conte Cañon to Grouse Meadow and the mouth of Palisade Creek; thence easterly up Palisade Creek Valley and over the pass between the waters of Palisade Creek and the drainage of the south fork of Kings River; thence through the Sequoia National Forest, Upper Basin, and traversing headwaters of the south fork of Kings River to the pass about one and one-half miles southwest of Mount Pinchot; thence southerly and southwesterly along Woods Creek and the south fork of same; thence by the way of Rae Lake, Glenn Pass, Bullfrog Lake and Bubbs Creek to and over an unnamed pass near Junction Peak; thence into the watershed of Tyndall Creek, and over and along the high sandy plateau and to Crabtree Meadows; thence in a general easterly direction to Mount Whitney." *Sierra Club Bulletin*, X, 1916, pp. 86-87.

[64]For accounts of the trail building see issues of the *Sierra Club Bulletin*, generally the year following the date mentioned.

[65]*Sierra Club Bulletin*, X, 1916, p. 90.

[66]*Sierra Club Bulletin*, X, 1916, p. 91.

[67]*Sierra Club Bulletin*, X, 1917, p. 221.

[68]Supplementary letter to 1930 annual report of Sequoia National Park dated September 12, 1930, written by Superintendent John R. White.

SECTION 8

[1]Colby interview, op. cit.

[2]George W. Stewart, "The Yokut Indians of the Kaweah Region," *Sierra Club Bulletin*, XII, number 4, 1927, p. 392.

SECTION 9

[1]François E. Matthes, *Geologic History of the Yosemite Valley*, U. S. Geological Survey, Paper 160, Washington, 1930, p. 104.

[2]Chester R. Longwell and Richard F. Flint, *Introduction to Physical Geology*, N. Y., John Wiley, 1955, p. 132.

[3]Matthes, op. cit. Accompanying map of glacial and postglacial deposits in Yosemite Valley. (The moraines are obscured by the trees in the photograph to some extent.) The map is not only useful for its information on glaciation but a delightful, colorful engraving to hang on a wall and look at for its artistic merit.

SECTION 11

[1]Matthes, op. cit., p. 77.

[2]Ibid., pp. 114-115.

SECTION 12

[1]George Struble, "Ghost Forests," *Sierra Club Bulletin* (monthly number), February 1956, p. 14. 1963 figures from *1963 Needle Miner Project*, Yosemite National Park, California, p. 1.

[2]John Muir, *My First Summer in the Sierra*, N. Y., Houghton Mifflin [1916], p. 202-203.

[3]N. F. McClure, "Explorations Among the Cañons North of the Tuolumne River," *Sierra Club Bulletin*, I, May 1894, p. 182.

[4]Quoted in *1963 Needle Miner Project*, op. cit., page i of preface.

[5]Extracts from Report of Superintendent of Yosemite National Park, *Sierra Club Bulletin*, IX, Jan. 1914, p. 206.

[6]Journal Agr. Rep. 21(3):127 by J. E. Patterson, "Life History of Recurvaria milleri."

[7]Interview with Emil Ernst in Yosemite in 1955.

[8]*Forest Insect Conditions in California in 1954*, an official report of the California Forest Pest Control Action Council, Sacramento, Jan. 1955, p. 6. Also memorandum from Emil Ernst, 1955.

[9]$100,000 figure from George Struble during interview Dec. 20, 1961.

[10]Resumé of U. S. Fish and Wildlife Service findings (1963) from James O. Keith, research biologist, University of California, Davis.

[11]John H. Storer, *The Web of Life*, N. Y., New American Library [1956], p. 67.

[12]Storer, ibid., pp. 74-75.

[13]*Leopold Report to Secretary of the Interior*, quoted in Sierra Club Bulletin (monthly number), March 1963, p. 5.

[14]G. R. Struble 1960, "The Lodgepole Needle Miner," Progress Report of Biological Research in 1959. USDA, Forest Service Pacific Southwest Forest and Range Experiment Station, 40 pp. (unpublished).

[15]A. D. Telford 1961, "Lodgepole Needle Miner Parasites: Biological Control and Insecticides," *Journal of Economic Entomology*, 54(2):347-355. Also see *Audubon Magazine*, March-April, 1963.

[16]Letter from A. D. Telford, March 11, 1964.

[17]*Audubon Magazine*, March-April, 1963.

[18]Resumé of U. S. Fish and Wildlife Service findings (1963) from James O. Keith, University of California, Davis.

[19]Letter from James O. Keith, February 13, 1964.

[20]*Leopold Report*, op. cit., p. 9.

[21]David Brower, *Sierra Club Bulletin* (monthly number), September 1963, p. 12.

SECTION 13

[1]Lowell Sumner and Joseph S. Dixon, *Birds and Mammals of the Sierra Nevada*, Berkeley, University of California Press, 1935, p. 439.

[2]A. Starker Leopold, et alii, *The Jawbone Deer Herd*, Game Bulletin No. 4, California Department of Natural Resources, Division of Fish and Game, 1951, p. 62. Much of the following material is based on the Jawbone study. Regrettably this superb and fascinating little book is out of print and difficult to find. It should be re-issued — perhaps in popular form — and be made widely available, especially since it could be instrumental in changing many ill-advised present deer practices.

[3]William M. Longhurst, et alii, *Survey of California Deer Herds, Their Ranges and Management Problems*, Game Bulletin No. 6, California Department of Fish and Game, Bureau of Game Conservation, p. 12; p. 74.

[4]A. Starker Leopold, et alii, op. cit., p. 112. Also memorandum from Robert D. Metherell, Yosemite biologist, regarding pellet census of the Clark herd which works out to the same percentage.

[5]Lowell Sumner and Joseph S. Dixon, op. cit., p. 451.

SECTION 14

[1]L. Don Leet and Sheldon Judson, *Physical Geology*, New Jersey, Prentice-Hall [1962], Chapt. 12. An excellent introduction to glaciation. Also see Joseph Le Conte (the elder), "Ramblings Through the High Sierra," *Sierra Club Bulletin*, III, Jan. 1900, pp. 57-64. An interesting account of glaciation written in 1875. Also see Chester R. Longwell and Richard Foster Flint, *Introduction to Physical Geology*, N. Y., John Wiley, p. 193.

[2]L. Don Leet and Sheldon Judson, op. cit., p. 248.

[3]A. E. Harrison, *Exploring Glaciers—with a Camera*, San Francisco, Sierra Club, p. 9.

SECTION 15

[1]Roderick Peattie, *The Sierra Nevada: The Range of Light*, N. Y., Vanguard Press [1947], p. 308.

[2]Milton S. Ray, "Discovery of the Nest and Eggs of the Gray-Crowned Leucosticte," *Sierra Club Bulletin*, VIII, Jan. 1911, pp. 34-38.

[3]William Leon Dawson, *The Birds of California*, San Diego, South Moulton Company, 1923, Vol. I, p. 156. Lowell Sumner and Joseph S. Dixon, *Birds and Mammals of the Sierra Nevada*, Berkeley, Univ. of Calif. Press, 1953, pp. 231-234. Also observation by R. N. McIntyre, August 3, 1949, on file at the Yosemite Museum.

[4]Observation by W. L. Neely, August 1953, on file at the Yosemite Museum.

[5]Vernon Bailey, "Animal Friends of the High Sierra," *Sierra Club Bulletin*, XVII, Feb. 1932, p. 22.

[6]Lowell Sumner and Joseph S. Dixon, op. cit., p. 233.

[7]Roderick Peattie, op. cit., p. 309.

[8]Orland Bartholomew, "A Winter in the High Sierra," *Sierra Club Bulletin*, XV, Feb. 1930, p. 70.

SECTION 16

[1]This material is based on François R. Matthes, *Geologic History of the Yosemite Valley*, U. S. Geological Survey Professorial Paper 160, Washington, 1930, and a chapter by Matthes in *The Sierra Nevada* by Roderick Peattie, N. Y., Vanguard [1947]. Also see M. E. Beatty, *Geology of Yosemite Valley*, Yosemite Nature Notes, Vol. XXII, No. 4.

[2]For geological dating see Chester R. Longwell and Richard F. Flint, *Introduction to Physical Geology*, N. Y., John Wiley [1955], Chapter 4. Also "Pre-Cambrian," *Encyclopaedia Britannica* [1953], Vol. XVIII, p. 426a.

SECTION 18

[1]Memorandum from William C. Putnam

[2]See François Matthes, *Marks of Time*, San Francisco, Sierra Club [1962], pp. 101-108; Richard J. Hartesvelt, *Devil Postpile National Monument*, Yosemite Nature Notes, Vol. XXX, No. 10; and Norman E. A. Hinds, *Evolution of the California Landscape*, San Francisco, Department of Natural Resources, Division of Mines, Bulletin 158, 1952, pp. 57, 60. For discussion of Devils Postpile. L. Don Leet and Sheldon Judson, *Physical Geology*, New Jersey, Prentice-Hall [1962], Chap. 5 (especially last part) present a good discussion of theory involved.

SECTION 19

[1]David S. Jordan and H. W. Henshaw, *Report of the Chief Engineers, U. S. Army*, 1878, pp. 1616-1617, as quoted in B. W. Evermann, Bulletin of the Bureau of Fisheries, XXV, 1905, p. 26.

[2]Quoted in Evermann, ibid., p. 33.

[3]Leo Shapovalov, et allii, "A Revised Check List of the Freshwater and Anadromous Fishes of California," California Fish and Game, Vol. 45(3), July, 1959.

[4]Evermann, op. cit., p. 22.

[5]Old volcanic eruptions have changed the drainage pattern of Volcano Creek (later named Golden Trout Creek) from the main Kern River to the South Fork and back again. In 1883 the Board of Supervisors of Tulare County granted permission for certain ranchers to increase the flow of irrigation water in the drainage of the South Fork by tunneling to nearby Volcano Creek which was slightly higher. The first tunnel caved in and was changed to an open cut which stopped running about 1899.

[6]J. H. Wales, *Trout of California*, Dept. of Fish and Game, 1957, p. 17.

[7]Evermann, op. cit., section of the 1905 study entitled "Temperature Conditions in the Kern River Region," by O. P. Jenkins. Also a letter from Alex Calhoun of the Dept. of Fish and Game dated March 12, 1964.

[8]Brian Curtis, "The Golden Trout of Cottonwood Lakes" Transactions of the American Fisheries Society, 1934, p. 261. Also memoranda from Alex Calhoun, March 12, 1964.

[9]Wales, op. cit., p. 52.

[10]Curtis, op. cit., p. 263.

SECTION 21

[1]See Harold Gilliam, "Hickory-Winged Mountaineers Vs. the Fireside Sloths," *San Francisco Examiner*, January 29, 1961; Weldon F. Heald, "Sierra Snows—Past and Future," *Sierra Club Bulletin*, XXXIV, June 1949, p. 56; Roderick Peattie, *Sierra Nevada: The Range of Light*, N. Y., Vanguard Press [1947], pp. 323-340; François E. Matthes, *The Incomparable Valley*, Berkeley, Univ. of Calif. Press, 1950, pp. 36-37; a letter (March 9, 1964) from C. Robert Elford, state climatologist, gives slightly lower snow records.

[2]Orland Bartholomew, "A Winter in the High Sierra," *Sierra Club Bulletin*, XV, Feb. 1930, pp. 69-73. A far too short account of a fantastic adventure.

[3]Harold Gilliam, *Weather of the San Francisco Bay Region*, Berkeley, Univ. of Calif. Press, 1962. A handy little guide to Northern California weather, well-written, illustrated, and easy to follow. Reading list at end.

[4]Roderick Peattie, op. cit., p. 336.

SECTION 22 (Seven Gables)

[1]Theodore S. Solomons, "A Search for a High Mountain Route from the Yosemite to the King's River Cañon," *Sierra Club Bulletin* I, May, 1895, p. 230.

SECTION 24

[1]Estimate in Dec. 1963 from Glenn Burns, widely experienced packer.

[2]It is extremely difficult to find much in the way of reliable packing statistics, for its practitioners tend to have little appreciation of industry-wide studies and trends. Most of the information is from personal interviews. Also see Norman B. Livermore, Jr., "Sierra Packing and Wilderness Policy," *Sierra Club Bulletin*, XXXII, May 1947, pp. 96-98.

[3]*A Back Country Management Plan for Sequoia and Kings Canyon National Parks*, Washington, U. S. Department of the Interior, 1963, figure 2.

[4]The Sierra packing associations might well hire some expert public relations people to tell Californians about the Sierra Nevada and the packing business, for most Californians have little idea of the size and magnificence of the mountains or that a packing business even exists. The most profitable trips are large riding parties with one or more packers and a cook. Such trips might be promoted after Labor Day.

SECTION 28

[1]Fire is not a factor in the perpetuation of high altitude meadows.

[2]*A Back Country Management Plan for Sequoia and Kings Canyon National Parks*, Washington, U. S. Department of the Interior, 1963, pp. 16-22.

[3]Carl W. Sharsmith, *A Report of the Status, Changes, and Ecology of Back Country Meadows in Sequoia and Kings Canyon National Parks*, U. S. National Park Service, July 23, 1958.

[4]Ibid., concluding section.

[5]Arnold P. Snyder, *Wilderness Area Management*: An Administrative Study of a Portion of the High Sierra Wilderness Area, U. S. Department of Agriculture, Region 5, Forest Service, 1960, p. 1. Also interview with author.

[6]E. Lowell Sumner, Jr., *Special Report on Range Management and Wildlife Protection*, U. S. National Park Service, 1940.

[7]Paul A. Zahl, "Plants That Eat Insects," *National Geographic*, May, 1961, pp. 642-659.

SECTION 29

[1]Chester Versteeg, "The Peaks and Passes of the Upper Basin, South Fork of the Kings River," *Sierra Club Bulletin*, XI, 1923, p. 423.

[2]J. S. Hutchinson, "A New Link in the John Muir Trail; Palisade Creek-Mather Pass," *Sierra Club Bulletin*, XI, 1923, p. 358.

[3]Versteeg, op. cit., p. 424; also see Hutchinson, op. cit., p. 363.

[4]Francis P. Farquhar, "The First Ascent of the Middle Palisade," *Sierra Club Bulletin*, XI, 1922, p. 270.

[5]Hutchinson, op. cit., p. 367.

SECTION 31 (Twin Lakes)

[1]Padre Pedro Font, *Diary* (edited by Herbert E. Bolton), quoted in *California Place Names*, by Erwin G. Gudde, Univ. of Calif. Press, 1960, p. 293.

[2]The Sierra Club, A Handbook, San Francisco, 1951, p. 41.

SECTION 33

[1]Erwin G. Gudde, *California Place Names*, Berkeley, Univ. of Calif. Press, 1960. The authoritative book on California place names.

[2]François E. Matthes, *The Incomparable Valley*, Berkeley, Univ. of Calif. Press, 1950, p. 118 and plate 11.

[3]Tracy I. Storer and Robert L. Usinger, *Sierra Nevada Natural History*, Berkeley, Univ. of Calif. Press, 1963, p. 51.

SECTION 34

[1]P. Ferry, "Invincible Skypilot," *American Forests*, August 1951, p. 28.

SECTION 36

[1]Specimens collected near Mt. Baxter in 1911 by Carr for the Museum of Vertebrate Zoology, as quoted in Fred L. Jones, "Survey of the Sierra Nevada Bighorn," *Sierra Club Bulletin*, XXXV, June 1950, p. 46.

[2]Ralph E. Welles and Florence B. Welles, *Bighorn of Death Valley*, Washington, U. S. Government Printing Office, 1961, p. 141.

[3]Lowell Sumner and Joseph S. Dixon, *Birds and Mammals of the Sierra Nevada*, Berkeley, University of California Press, 1953, p. 458.

[4]Joseph C. Wampler, *Life History of Sierra Nevada Bighorn*, unpublished paper, Museum of Vertebrate Zoology, University of California, Berkeley, p. 3.

[5]Jones, op. cit., p. 64.

[6]Welles, op. cit., p. 112.

[7]Welles, ibid., p. 101.

[8]Sumner and Dixon, op. cit., p. 458.

[9]Sumner and Dixon, ibid., p. 456.

[10]Frank Stephens, *California Mammals*, San Diego, West Coast Publishing Co., 1906, p. 351. J. A. Allen, "Historical and nomenclatorial notes on North American sheep," *Bulletin, Am. Mus. Nat. Hist.*, v. XXXI, pp.1-29, quoted in Wampler, op. cit., p. 11.

[11]Sumner and Dixon (p. 461) record bighorn poaching in 1935. A letter (Feb. 10, 1964) from Gene Gerdes, California Dept. of Fish and Game, details the 1954 killing of a bighorn ram on San Joaquin Mt.

[12]Jones, op. cit., p. 43.

[13]Jones, ibid., p. 73. Also see Leopold Report to the Secretary of the Interior, *Sierra Club Bulletin* (monthly number) March, 1963, p. 7.

[14]*The Ranger*, U. S. Forest Service, quoted in Sumner and Dixon, op. cit., p. 460.

SECTION 38

[1]"Conifers in Cultivation," *Conifer Conference, London, Report*. Royal Horticultural Society, 1932, pp. 203-204.

SECTION 39

[1]François E. Matthes, "The Geologic History of Mount Whitney," *Sierra Club Bulletin*, XXII, Feb. 1937, p. 6.

[2]Francis P. Farquhar traces the early history of Whitney in three superbly documented articles, "The Story of Mount Whitney," *Sierra Club Bulletin*, XIV, Feb. 1929, p. 39; XX, Feb. 1935, p. 81; XXI, Feb. 1936, p. 64.

[3]Sierra Club Bulletin, V, Jan. 1905, p. 259.

[4]C. G. Abbot, "A Shelter for Observers on Mount Whitney," *Smithsonian Miscellaneous Collections*, 1910, Vol. 52, No. 1886, p. 505, as quoted by Farquhar, op. cit., Feb. 1936, p. 68.

[5]Letter from Professor McAdie to Francis P. Farquhar, Nov. 5, 1935, as quoted by Farquhar, op. cit., Feb. 1936, p. 70.

[6]C. G. Abbot, "Report on the Astrophysical Observatory," *Annual Report of the Board of Regents of the Smithsonian Institution, for 1911*, p. 62, as quoted by Farquhar, op. cit., Feb. 1936, p. 71.

[7]See Andrew Hamilton and Chandler Harris, "Big, Busy Mountain," *Saturday Evening Post*, May 12, 1956.

SECTION 40

[1]*Life*, Oct. 19, 1962, p. 69.

[2]*A Back Country Management Plan for Sequoia and Kings Canyon National Parks*, Washington, U. S. Department of the Interior, 1963, figure 2.

[3]Letter from William J. Briggle, district ranger, Sequoia-Kings Canyon National Park, to Chief Ranger, dated March 26, 1958.

[4]Letter from Ranger Buck S. Brant to Sierra district ranger, dated Feb. 18, 1963.

[5]Interview with Ranger Arn Snyder in Dec. 1963.

[6]*A Back Country Management Plan for Sequoia and Kings Canyon National Parks*, op. cit., p. 9.

[7]Arnold P. Snyder, "How Wild the Wilderness," *American Forests*, May 1961, as quoted in *A Back Country Management Plan for Sequoia and Kings Canyon National Parks*, op. cit., p. 9.

Index

(° indicates illustration)

Wenz, Mike, 136
westernbog blueberry, 144
Western Mono Indians, 50-51
Weyl, agriculturalist, 16
Wheeler, George M., 13
White, Stewart Edward, 99; — W. House, the, 23; — W. Mountains, 207
Whitney, Joseph D., 10, 13, 21, 209; — W.Creek, 210-211*; — W. Portal, 214; — W. Survey Party, 10-13, 36, 134; — W. Trail, 214 (see also Mt. Whitney)

wilderness, 217-218
Winchell, Lil A., 134
Wisconsin, 19; — W. ice age, 61, 94
Wood, A. E., 17
Woods Creek, 33, 40, 53, 166*-169*, 205
Woodworth Mountain, 39
World War I, 17; — World War II, 132, 141, 156, 177, 184
Wynne, S. N., 44

— X —
xenolith, 150-151*

— Y —
Yale University, 13, 24
Yokut Indians, 50, 53
Yosemite, the Yosemite, Yosemite Valley, 10-12, 15-16, 20, 23-28, 32, 38-39, 41, 47-48, 51, 53, 57, 61, 63-70, 73, 75-76, 83, 109, 126, 131, 184, 217-218; — Y. *Guide Book*, 21; — Y. National Park, 10, 16-17, 23, 41-42, 70, 75; — Y. Park & Curry Co., 57

— Z —
zoology, zoologist, 126, 175